Records of Achievement

YEAR 1

SCOTTISH PRIMARY 2

Credits

Authors Elaine Hampton and Karen Leigh

Editor David Sandford

Assistant Editors Roanne Charles and Clare Gallaher

Series Designers Rachel O'Kane and Lynne Joesbury

Designer Erik Ivens

Cover illustration John-Paul Early

Illustrations Frazer Worth

Published by Scholastic Ltd,
Villiers House,
Clarendon Avenue,
Leamington Spa,
Warwickshire CV32 5PR

Printed by Bell & Bain Ltd, Glasgow

1 2 3 4 5 6 7 8 9 0   4 5 6 7 8 9 0 1 2 3

British Library Cataloguing-in-Publication Data
A catalogue record for this book is available from the British Library.

ISBN 0-439-98327-4

Contents

Introduction

Assessing a child's progress is a necessary part of school life for children and teachers alike. There are two types of assessment: formal assessment at the end of each key stage (SATs), and teacher assessment, both ongoing and end-of-key-stage. Written reports for parents or carers, detailing an individual child's progress and achievements, should be sent home at least once a year.

Reporting and teacher assessment need to be based on evidence, which should be drawn from a child's practical work and from classroom discussion. Records of achievement form another part of this evidence-gathering process, and are an excellent way of checking an individual's level of knowledge.

The *Records of Achievement* series provides photocopiable worksheets that can be integrated with children's own work and your existing scheme of work, adding breadth and variety; or alternatively could be used as the sole record of achievement. By using these worksheets at the end of a topic or unit of study, you can integrate purposeful application of knowledge and skills, differentiation, assessment and record-keeping.

About this book

Curriculum coverage

Each book in the series can be used to provide evidence of progress in the following subject areas:

- science
- history
- geography
- information and communication technology
- art and design
- music
- design and technology
- religious education
- PSHE and citizenship.

English and maths are not included in this series because we feel that most schools already keep comprehensive records in these subjects, including SATs at Year 2 and Year 6, and the optional SATs at Years 3, 4 and 5.

Each activity corresponds to a unit in the QCA Schemes of Work for Year 1. They should therefore be used once a unit of work has been completed. As there is currently no Scheme of Work for PSHE, the content of this section is based on appropriate key areas of study.

Unlike the prescriptive nature of the Schemes of Work for maths and English, teaching other subjects very much depends on how you want to focus particular areas of work. The *Records of Achievement* series is relevant to Scottish schools, and those not following the QCA Schemes, as the worksheets relate to the programmes of study most schools would be teaching in any case.

Teacher's notes

There are brief teacher's notes to accompany each activity, providing guidance on the vocabulary the children should have become familiar with in completing the QCA unit, and a brief résumé of what will need to have been studied in order to complete the relevant worksheets.

Differentiated worksheets

There are at least three differentiated worksheets provided for each activity. These are based on the 'end of unit expectations' for the corresponding unit in the QCA Schemes of Work. The level of expectation for each sheet is indicated with ✔ symbols:

✔ for children who have not made so much progress
✔✔ for what most children will have achieved
✔✔✔ for children who have progressed further.

By differentiating the activities in this way, all children can make an appropriate record of their achievement, regardless of ability, at the end of a unit of study. If appropriate, children could complete more than one worksheet for each activity, depending on their level of knowledge and understanding, as each worksheet builds on the previous one.

The worksheets are designed for children to work on independently. However, the accompanying teacher's notes provide a general introduction to provide a context for the activity before the children begin work. Some children may require support with reading the sheets, but it is important that they work independently to complete the tasks.

Record-keeping

At the bottom of each worksheet is an 'I can...' statement based on the expectations as set out in the relevant QCA unit of study. Once they have completed the sheet satisfactorily, the child can tick the box following the statement; you can then use this information to provide evidence of assessment, and to begin to build up a comprehensive record of an individual's achievements.

Science

Science provides children with the opportunity to develop their knowledge and understanding, developing curiosity about things they observe and experience, and encourages them to explore the world about them with all their senses. They should begin to acquire and refine skills of investigation, develop language skills through talking about their work, and develop a respect for the environment and living things and their own health and safety.

In Year 1, children study the following: 'Ourselves' (identifying parts of the body and living things); 'Growing plants' (identifying the parts of a plant and conditions for growth); 'Sorting and using materials' (naming and describing different materials); 'Light and dark' (knowing about the dangers of looking directly at the Sun and that light is needed to see); 'Pushes and pulls' (identifying types of movement); and 'Sound and hearing' (learning that we hear with our ears).

Ourselves

Unit 1A

✔ **Learning outcomes** (page 12)
To locate parts of the body. To make comparisons.

✔✔ **Learning outcome** (page 13)
To identify the five senses and distinguish their purposes.

✔✔✔ **Learning outcome** (page 14)
To identify animals as living things which feed, move and use their senses.

In this unit children will learn, through exploring and using their senses and by observing and describing living things, that humans and other animals are living things that move and grow. Children should be able to identify common features of living things and make comparisons between living and non-living things, considering how to treat living things with care and sensitivity.

When working on this unit, make sure the children are familiar with particular words and phrases relating to: senses, parts of the body, living and non-living things, making comparisons and scientific ideas (*head, eye, arm, sight, see, hear, smell, leg, wing, arm, beak, alive, living, human, tall/taller/tallest, describe*).

Photocopiable page 12 requires children to have located and named parts of the body (such as arm, leg, knee, eye, mouth) on themselves and others. For photocopiable page 13, they will need to be able to identify the names of the five senses and the organs associated with them, for example: *the nose is for smelling, the tongue is for tasting.* Ask the children completing photocopiable page 14 to identify differences between living and non-living things; they should be able to tell you that human beings are animals, and that all animals are living things that have certain requirements in terms of food, water and so on.

Growing plants

Unit 1B

✔ **Learning outcome** (page 15)
To identify parts of a plant and its need for water.

✔✔ **Learning outcome** (page 16)
To identify parts of a plant and the conditions it needs to grow.

✔✔✔ **Learning outcome** (page 17)
To find out by experimenting what plants require to grow well.

In this unit children will become aware, through experimenting and investigating, of what plants require to grow and change; they should have the opportunity to record observations and draw conclusions.

You should make sure that the children are familiar with words and phrases relating to: making comparisons relating to plants, and living and non-living things (*leaf, stem, petal, root, flower, healthy/unhealthy, tall/taller, similar to, different from, branch, living, non-living*).

Photocopiable page 15 assesses whether children can identify and name the main parts of a plant, and whether they know what a plant needs to grow. To complete photocopiable page 16, children will also need to consider that a plant is a living thing and requires certain things to continue to grow healthily. Provide opportunities for children to investigate what are good conditions for plants to grow in and what are poor conditions for plants to grow in – this should lead to the conclusion that plants need to be treated with care and sensitivity. Photocopiable page 17 encourages children to observe differences between plants growing in different conditions, and to record their findings.

Sorting and using materials

Unit 1C

✔ **Learning outcome** (page 18)
To recognise the materials some objects are made from.

✔✔ **Learning outcome** (page 19)
To recognise common materials and describe their properties.

✔✔✔ **Learning outcome** (page 20)
To say why a material is suitable for a particular purpose.

This unit asks children to experiment with different materials, and to think about their properties and what they might be useful for. They should be able to identify specific properties of a material, and be able to think about why these properties might make the material suitable for a particular job, thinking of possible ways to test their ideas.

Children will need to become familiar with vocabulary to describe a material and its properties (*wood, metal, plastic, paper, glass, stone, rubber, wool, fabric, hard/soft, rough/ smooth, transparent, shiny*), and with vocabulary for making comparisons and giving reasons for choices (*because, better, different from, harder*).

Photocopiable page 18 asks children to identify objects made from each of three different materials. Encourage them to describe the objects using appropriate vocabulary and to say how they know what each is made of. Photocopiable page 19 extends this by asking children to think about specific properties of different objects and to group objects based on different characteristics. Children could use the properties of objects to think about why they are made from a particular material, and to consider why a material is chosen for a specific purpose on the basis of their properties. This allows for some experimentation – for example, testing for being waterproof or absorbent. Photocopiable page 20 allows children to write about the suitability of materials for a purpose, and to state reasons for their choice.

Light and dark

Unit 1D

✔ **Learning outcomes** (page 21)
To recognise that you cannot see in the dark. To know that it is dangerous to look directly at the Sun. To be able to name a number of light sources.

✔✔ **Learning outcomes** (page 22)
To recognise that you cannot see in the dark. To know that it is dangerous to look directly at the Sun. To be able to describe and compare light sources.

✔✔✔ **Learning outcome** (page 23)
To know and explain that we cannot see shiny objects in the dark because they are not light sources.

Following this unit, children should develop, through experimentation and investigation, an understanding of the need for light in order to see things. They will discover that 'darkness' is the absence of light, and that without light we cannot see any object. Children should also be encouraged to notice that there are many sources of light around us, including the Sun. It is important to stress to the children that they should never look directly at the Sun.

In work on light and dark, children should be able to name different light sources (*Sun, torch, candle, lamp*) and be able to use the vocabulary of comparison when looking at different light sources (*bright/brighter/brightest, dark/darker/darkest*), giving reasons for their ideas.

The worksheets in this activity require the children to have experience of a 'dark area', which should demonstrate that without light we are unable to see. Photocopiable page 21 reinforces safety in relation to never looking at the Sun, and encourages children to identify and name other sources of light around them. Encourage them to look for unusual light sources, and to think about which is the brightest. Comparing the brightness of different light sources provides useful vocabulary practice – photocopiable page 22 allows children to begin to compare different light sources. Some children may want to investigate shiny objects, finding out how easy it is to see them in the dark – they should discover that without any light, even shiny objects can't be seen. Photocopiable page 23 provides an opportunity to investigate what makes an object shiny. Take every opportunity to remind the children of the danger of looking directly at the Sun.

Pushes and pulls

Unit 1E

✔ **Learning outcome** (page 24)
To observe and describe movements made by themselves and other objects.

✔✔ **Learning outcome** (page 25)
To observe, describe and compare movements in terms of speed and direction.

✔✔✔ **Learning outcome** (page 26)
To understand how the wind can make things move.

Work in this unit will introduce children to different sorts of movement, and will encourage them to relate these movements to pushes and pulls through experimentation and investigation. Children should know how to make objects start and stop moving safely by using a push or a pull, and use vocabulary to describe movement in terms of speed and direction.

Before working on these sheets, you will need to make sure that the children are comfortable using vocabulary relating to movement and direction (*push, pull*) and of comparison (*faster, slower, further*), being able to give reasons for their answers.

Photocopiable page 24 focuses on objects that can be pushed and pulled, and asks children to identify everyday objects around them that require a push or a pull to make them move. Photocopiable page 25 extends this by asking children to think about the direction of movement when an object is pushed or pulled; they should also be able to describe how an object can be made to slow down or speed up. More able children can investigate the power of wind as a force, looking at how far they can blow a selection of small objects. In each case, the children should be able to identify the wind as the cause of motion. Encourage these children to predict what will happen, and to record their findings on photocopiable page 26.

Sound and hearing

Unit 1F

✔ **Learning outcomes** (page 27)
To recognise that we hear with our ears. To recognise, describe and record different sounds.

✔✔ **Learning outcomes** (page 28)
To recognise that we hear with our ears. To relate sounds to specific objects. To observe what happens when you move further away.

✔✔✔ **Learning outcome** (page 29)
To recognise that when an object makes a sound something moves or vibrates.

Through listening to sounds and making sounds themselves, children should develop their understanding of sound and be able to identify sources of sounds they encounter. Experimental work should help them understand that sound radiates from a point, and gets quieter as it travels further away from the source. Their work should provide opportunities for children to relate understanding of sound and hearing to everyday experiences, for example identifying the sounds they can hear around the classroom and where they come from.

When looking at sound, children should be familiar with vocabulary describing sounds or ways of making sounds (*loud, quiet, shake, pluck, rattle, ring, silence, direction*), and should be able to make comparisons between sounds (*louder/quieter, further away/nearer*) using near-synonyms (*soft/quiet, noise/sound*), and identify words which have different meanings in other contexts (*low, high, soft*).

These worksheets require the children to have experienced many different sources of sound, and for them to have made observations about the sounds they can hear by listening carefully. When completing photocopiable page 27, the children should identify objects around them that make sounds, and begin to understand why some sounds are louder than others. Photocopiable page 28 asks children to match sounds to their sources, and to think about what happens when sounds get further away. You might like to ask pairs of children to investigate this practically. Some children could try making instruments to see how sounds are made – can they identify that it is the vibrating part of the instrument that is making the sound? Photocopiable page 29 helps them to think about this.

Name ______________________ Date ______________

Ourselves

- Draw lines to label the parts of the body.

head

eye

arm

leg

knee

nose

mouth

hand

foot

- Colour in the sentences that are true.

Human beings are animals.

People need to eat to stay healthy.

All people have brown eyes.

Record of Achievement *I can name the parts of the body and describe some aspects of humans.* ☐

Name ______________________________ Date ____________________

Ourselves

- Draw lines to label the parts of the body.
- Circle the words that you use for your senses.

head

eye

arm

leg

knee

nose

mouth

hand

foot

- Complete these sentences. The first has been done for you.

The *ear* is for hearing.

The __________________ is for seeing.

The __________________ is for tasting.

The __________________ is for smelling.

The __________________ is for touching.

Record of Achievement *I can name parts of the body including the sense organs.* ☐

Name ____________________ Date ____________

Ourselves

- Draw three living things and three non-living things in the boxes below.

Living things

Non-living things

- Write down three things that can be said about all living things.

____

____

____

Record of Achievement

I can describe living things. ☐

Name ______________________ Date ______________

Growing plants

- Label the parts of this plant. Use the words in the box.

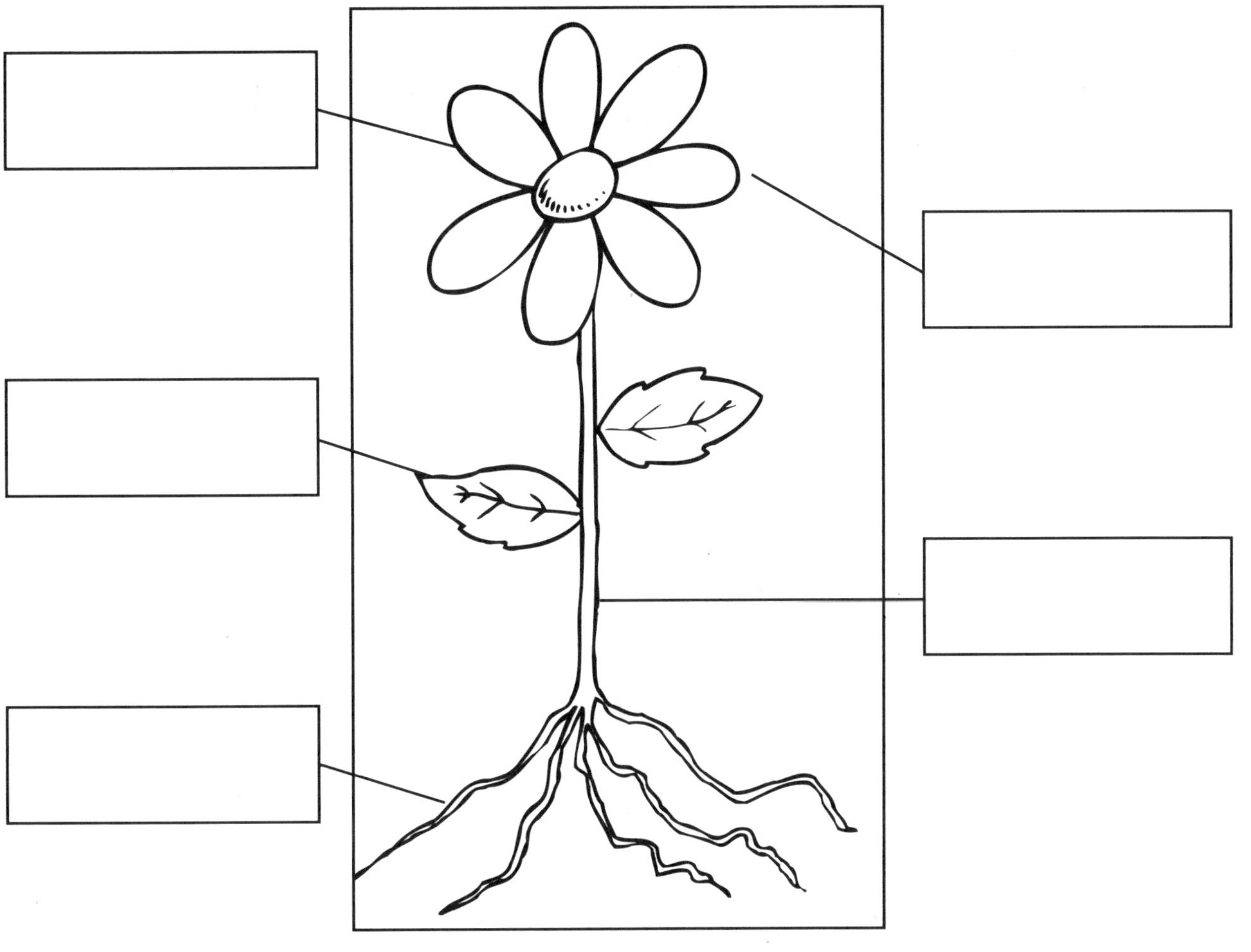

leaf	stem	root	flower	petal

- Write a sentence saying what all plants need in order to grow.

____

____

Record of Achievement

I can label the parts of a plant. ☐

Name ______________________ Date ______________

Growing plants

- Label the parts of this plant. Use the words in the box.

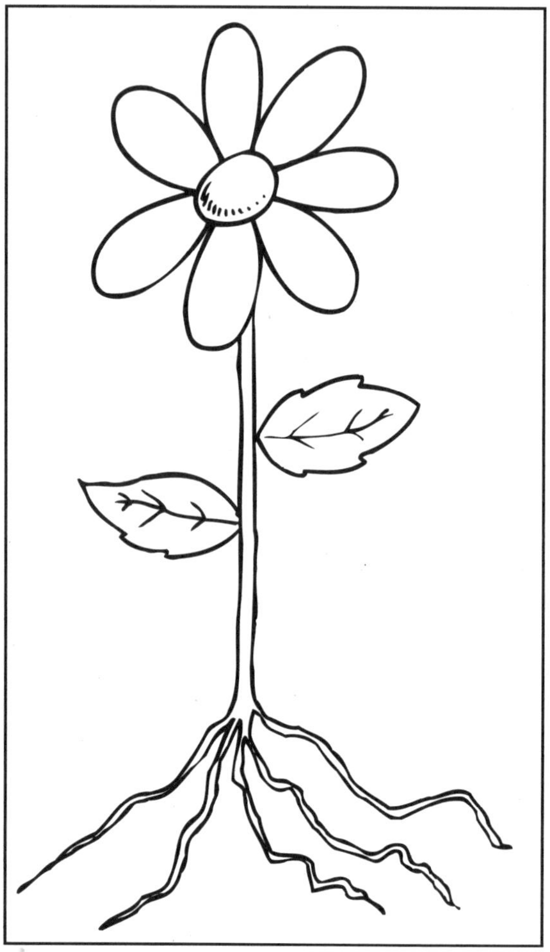

leaf	stem	root	flower	petal

- Write two or three sentences to say how you would care for a plant to keep it healthy.

____

____

____

Record of Achievement

I can label the parts of a plant and know how to keep a plant healthy. ☐

Name ______________________ Date ______________

Growing plants

- Look closely at these two plants. One was grown on a windowsill and the other was grown in a cupboard.
- Put a tick next to the one that was grown on a windowsill.

- Describe the differences between the two plants.

____

____

____

____

- Why is the plant that grew in the cupboard unhealthy?

____

____

____

Record of Achievement *I can describe what plants need to grow well.* ☐

Name ______________________ Date ______________

Sorting and using materials

- Find and draw three things made from wood.

- Find and draw three things made from metal.

- Find and draw three things made from plastic.

Record of Achievement

I can recognise wood, metal and plastic objects. ☐

Name ______________________ Date ______________

Sorting and using materials

- Read the sentence in each box. Find an object that matches the description.
- Draw the object and complete the sentence.

This is hard. It is made from ____________	This is soft. It is made from ____________
This is rough. It is made from ____________	This is smooth. It is made from ____________
This is transparent. It is made from ____________	This is shiny. It is made from ____________

Record of Achievement

I can use words to describe materials and objects. ☐

Name ______________________ Date ______________

Sorting and using materials

● Which materials would be best to make these things? Choose from the words at the bottom of the page.

	Material	Why you think this is best
A bird table 		
A saucepan 		
A window 		
An envelope 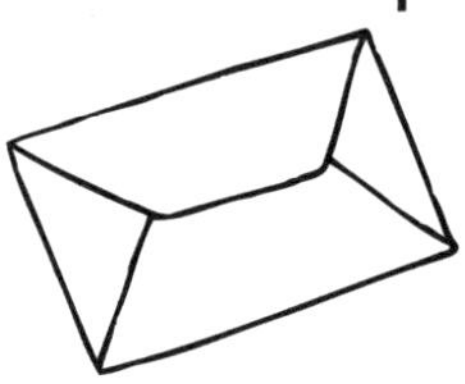		

paper glass stone plastic fabric
wood rubber metal wool

Record of Achievement

I can say why I would choose a particular material for an object. ☐

Name ______________________ Date ______________

Light and dark

The Sun is our main source of light.
It can be dangerous.

- **You must never** ______________________

____

____

- Draw three other sources of light and label them.

______ ______ ______

Record of Achievement

I know that the Sun can be dangerous. I can name three sources of light. ☐

Name ______________________ Date ______________

Light and dark

The Sun is our main source of light. It can be dangerous.

- **You must never** ________________________________

____

- Draw and label five different sources of light.

- Put a tick next to the brightest light source.

Record of Achievement *I know that the Sun can be dangerous. I can say which light source is the brightest.* ☐

Name ____________________ Date ____________

Light and dark

- Put a ring round the shiny objects

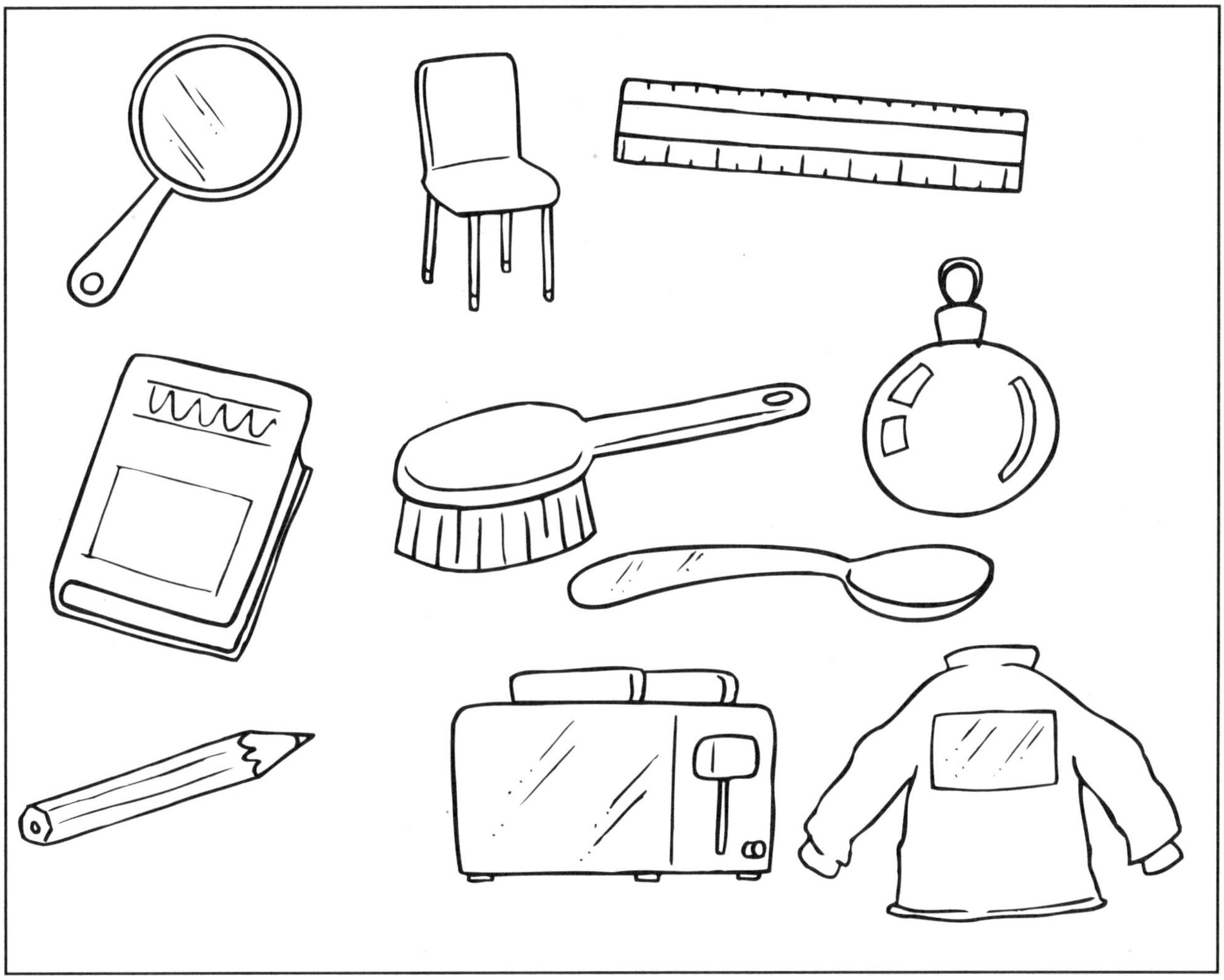

- What makes shiny objects shine? ____________________

____

- If the shiny objects are put in a dark room, what will happen to them? ____________________

____

Record of Achievement

I can talk about shiny objects. ☐

Name ______________________ Date ______________

Pushes and pulls

- Colour in **red** the things that can be moved by **pushing**.
- Colour in **blue** the things that can be moved by **pulling**.

• Draw another object that can be moved by pushing.	• Draw another object that can be moved by pulling.

Record of Achievement *I can identify objects that can be moved by pushing and pulling.* ☐

Name ______________________ Date ______________

Pushes and pulls

Always remember that some moving objects can be dangerous!

- The girl pushes the pram. Which way will the pram move? Draw an arrow.

- The girl pulls the pram. Which way will the pram move? Draw an arrow.

- How could the girl make the pram move faster?

____

Record of Achievement *I can describe how an object will move and how to make it move faster.* ☐

Name ______________________ Date ______________

Pushes and pulls

Always remember that some moving objects can be dangerous!

- Draw four things that can be moved by the wind.

You will need a straw, a ping-pong ball, a toy car, a feather and a small box.

- If you use the straw to blow each of the other objects, which do you think will move the furthest?

____

- Now try blowing the objects across the table with the straw.
- Which did you blow the furthest?

____

Record of Achievement

I can show how wind power can move something. ☐

Name ______________________ Date ______________

Sound and hearing

- Colour the things that will make a sound.

- Listen carefully and draw four things you can hear in the classroom.

- Draw something that will make a loud sound.

- Draw something that will make a quiet sound.

Record of Achievement

I can recognise and describe sounds. ☐

Name ______________________________ Date ______________

Sound and hearing

- What sounds can you hear?

- Draw a line to match the child to the sound they can hear.
- Ask a friend to ring a bell. Keep moving further and further away from your friend as they ring the bell. What happens to the sound you hear?

____

____

Record of Achievement

I can identify objects that make different sounds. ☐

Name ______________________ Date ______________

Sound and hearing

- Look at these instruments.
- What do you do to them to make a sound? Write the correct word under each instrument.

pluck	blow	bang

- Make an instrument you can pluck. You will need some elastic bands and a box.
- Draw your instrument.

- Can you explain how your instrument makes a sound?

____

____

Record of Achievement

I know that something moves or vibrates to make a sound. ☐

History

History provides children with the opportunity to develop an understanding of interpreting the past. In Year 1, children have the opportunity to compare life today with the past, using everyday things such as toys, homes and holidays. There are many opportunities to use vocabulary associated with the passing of time, and children can find out about the past using a variety of different sources of information and representations.

How are our toys different from those in the past?

Unit 1

✔ **Learning outcome** (page 33)
To identify some differences between old toys and new toys.

✔✔ **Learning outcome** (page 34)
To write about the differences between modern day toys and toys from the past.

✔✔✔ **Learning outcome** (page 35)
To give reasons why we know a toy is from the past.

Work in this unit should introduce children to the concept of 'old' and 'new', and will encourage them to think about changes that have occurred within their own lifetime, and in the life of others in their family. There are a great many sources of information for this topic – first-hand recollections from friends or family are particularly useful, as are museum exhibits.

Children will need to be familiar with vocabulary to describe the passing of time (*old, new, modern*) and for comparing old and new items (*older/newer, oldest/newest*), and adjectives to describe the items they are looking at (*dirty, clean, broken, rusty*).

Photocopiable page 33 encourages the children to think about their own toys in terms of 'new' and 'old'. Ask children how long they have had the toy – what condition is it in when compared to an older toy: is it scratched, or not so clean? Experience of looking at toys, or pictures of toys, from the past and present would be useful before completing photocopiable pages 34 and 35. Ask the children to consider the similarities and differences between the 'old' and 'new' toys shown on the worksheets, and encourage them to use appropriate vocabulary to describe how they know something is from the past.

What were homes like a long time ago?

Unit 2

✔ **Learning outcome** (page 36)
To identify some different types of homes.

✔✔ **Learning outcome** (page 37)
To identify household objects from the past and describe how and where they were used.

✔✔✔ **Learning outcome** (page 38)
To make comparisons of homes from different periods.

When working through this unit, children have the chance to look for similarities and differences between modern day homes and those from the past. Comparison of homes and of household objects should help children to distinguish between old and new, and help them to think about what life might have been like in the past.

Useful vocabulary for these activities relates to different types of house (for example, *detached, semi-detached, terrace, bungalow*), names of household objects (*iron, jug, kettle, washboard, washing machine, cooker*), and the language of time and comparison (*new, old, older, oldest, long ago, modern*).

Photocopiable page 36 requires the children to have had some experience of looking at homes from different periods – if there is a variety of architecture in the local area, this could be useful. Ask the children to consider the key features of different homes, both external and internal. When completing photocopiable page 37, children should have the opportunity to handle household objects from the past and be encouraged to talk about their uses, comparing them with the items that do a similar job today. Photocopiable page 38 encourages children to compare two different time periods, and think of reasons why some things would be found in a modern kitchen, but not in a kitchen from the past.

What were seaside holidays like in the past?

Unit 3

✔ **Learning outcome** (page 39)
To identify some features related to seaside holidays.

✔✔ **Learning outcome** (page 40)
To recognise some similarities and differences between holidays now and in the past.

✔✔✔ **Learning outcome** (page 41)
To write about holidays now and in the past and make comparisons between the two.

When working through this unit children will develop an understanding of chronology through comparing holidays past and present. These activities will encourage the children to develop their ability to use different sources of information to ask and answer questions about what life in the past might have been like.

Work on holidays and the seaside should encourage the children to use vocabulary related to geographical features (*seaside, sand, cliff, shingle, beach*), items for a seaside holiday (*windbreak, picnic, sun hat, sun cream, sunglasses, flip-flops, sandals*), and period-specific vocabulary (*steamboat, Punch and Judy show, amusement arcade, steam train, pier*) that allows comparison of time (*long ago, after the war, 1960s, recent, modern, older, oldest*).

Photocopiable page 39 encourages the children to think about the purpose of a holiday; talk with the children about this, and ask them to consider what items they might pack to take on holiday with them. They will need to have looked at photographs or pictures of holidays past and present, and started to use time-related vocabulary to discuss what they can see, when completing photocopiable pages 40 and 41, in order to compare a holiday taken a long time ago with one they might take today.

Name ______________________________ Date ___________________

How are our toys different from those in the past?

This is my newest toy.

This is my oldest toy.

- Complete these sentences about each of your toys.

My newest toy is a ______________________________

I know that this is my newest toy because ______________

____

My oldest toy is a ______________________________

I know that this is my oldest toy because ______________

____

Record of Achievement

I can identify old and new toys. ☐

Name ________________________________ Date ____________________

How are our toys different from those in the past?

- Put a ring round the modern toys.

- Write a sentence describing how these dolls are different.

____

____

____

Record of Achievement

I can write about the differences between modern toys and toys from the past. ☐

Name ______________________ Date ______________

How are our toys different from those in the past?

- Look at these toys. Write **old** or **new** by each one.

- Write a sentence saying how you can tell that the clockwork toy was made a long time ago.

____

____

____

Record of Achievement

I can explain how I know a toy was made a long time ago. ☐

Name ______________________ Date ______________

What were homes like a long time ago?

Here are some different types of homes.

detached house

semi-detached house

terraced house

bungalow

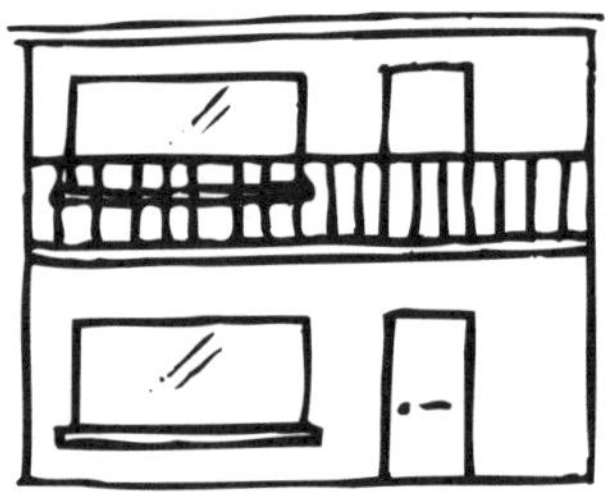

flat

- Draw a picture of your home and complete the sentences below.

My home is a ______________________________

It has ______________________________

Record of Achievement

I can recognise different types of homes. ☐

Name ______________________________ Date ___________________

What were homes like a long time ago?

- Match the household objects from the past and present.

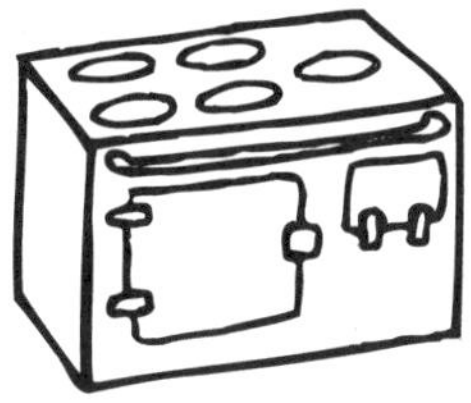

- In which room would you find these items?

____

- Draw a household object from the past that could be found in a living room.

Record of Achievement

I can recognise household objects from the past and present. ☐

Name ______________________ Date ______________

What were homes like a long time ago?

- Look at these two pictures. They show a kitchen from Victorian times and a modern kitchen.

- List five things that could be found in a modern kitchen that you would not find in a Victorian kitchen.

______________ ______________ ______________

______________ ______________

- Give a reason why these items could not be found in a Victorian kitchen.

____

____

Record of Achievement

I can compare homes past and present. ☐

Name ______________________________ Date ____________________

What were seaside holidays like in the past?

- Draw some things that you would take on a holiday to the seaside.

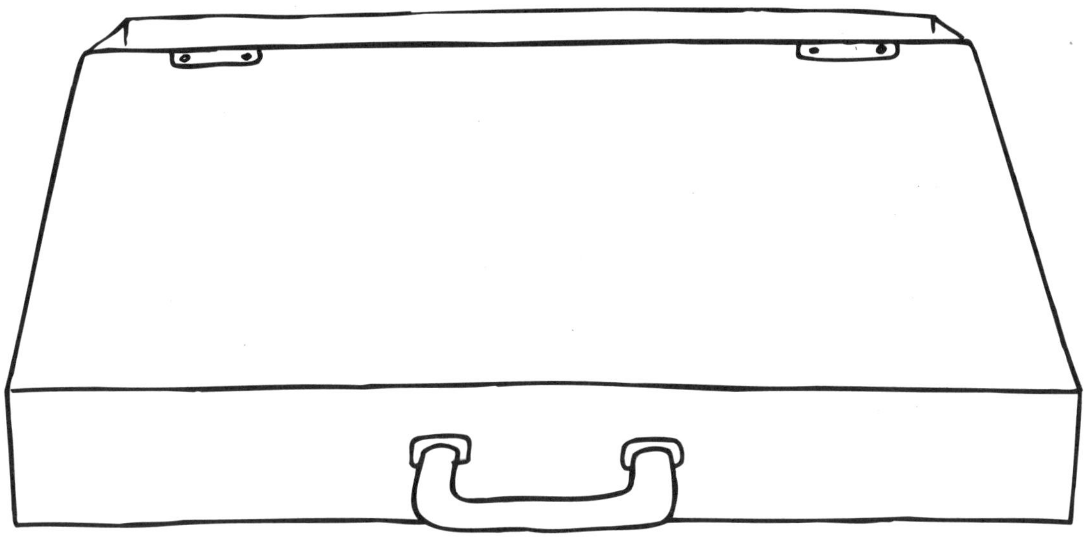

- Draw a picture of yourself at the seaside.
- Talk to your teacher about your picture.

Record of Achievement

I can talk about seaside holidays. ☐

Name ______________________ Date ______________

What were seaside holidays like in the past?

- Look at this seaside holiday picture from 100 years ago.

Punch and Judy	bucket and spade	pier
donkey ride	bathing hut	swimming costume

- Write some sentences about the picture. Use the words in the box to help you.

____

____

____

____

Record of Achievement

I can write about seaside holidays in the past. ☐

Name ______________________________ Date ____________________

What were seaside holidays like in the past?

- Look carefully at these two pictures and discuss with a friend how they are different.

- Tick the picture that shows a holiday from today.
- Write some sentences about how seaside holidays in the past were different to today's seaside holiday.

____

____

____

Record of Achievement

I can compare seaside holidays in the past with seaside holidays today. ☐

Geography

Geography in Year 1 is concerned with the study of people and places within the immediate local environment. It allows children to use their enquiry skills to make observations about people and places, and encourages them to form views and opinions about the environment and how it might be improved.

Around our school – the local area

Unit 1

✔ **Learning outcome** (page 45)
To recognise some of the features that make up the local area.

✔✔ **Learning outcome** (page 46)
To recognise a variety of features that make up the local area.

✔✔✔ **Learning outcome** (page 47)
To recognise features of the local area and suggest improvements.

Work in this unit should ideally take place over an extended period of time, allowing the children to explore their local area to identify notable features of their locality and to think about their uses. Children should consider why those features are required, or how they have come about. They should be encouraged to think about how the local area could be improved.

Work in the local environment allows the children to use vocabulary of maps and location (*address, near, far, travel, journey, routes, features*). Encourage them to identify buildings (*offices, church, shop, houses, flats, garage, factory, leisure centre, library, museum*) and places (*playground, park, parade*), and to form opinions about features of the locality, describing their thoughts and giving reasons for them.

Each of the photocopiable sheets in this unit requires the children to have developed a sense of place in relation to home and school. It will be useful if they can describe and draw their route to school, naming some of the main features they pass en route. (You will need to consider that some children will live in the locality but some may travel quite a distance to school.) Photocopiable pages 45 and 46 ask the children to look around them to identify local features of their environment, to understand how some of the features are used and to express views on those features. If possible, make reference to changes that have taken place in the local area. Photocopiable page 47 also asks children to think about the purpose of different buildings, and to suggest how the environment could be improved.

How can we make our local area safer?

Unit 2

✔ **Learning outcome** (page 48)
To suggest ideas for improving parking in the locality.

✔✔ **Learning outcomes** (page 49)
To carry out a local survey. To draw conclusions and discuss ways of tackling parking problems.

✔✔✔ **Learning outcomes** (page 50)
To carry out a local survey. To use the results to consider ways of tackling parking problems.

This unit is based around the problem of local parking. It asks the children to investigate the facilities for parking in school, and to think about ways in which it could be improved. This involves the children in some observational work which will lead to simple decision-making about how they might improve the quality of their environment.

This work allows the children to use vocabulary such as *traffic, survey, busy, quiet, street, parking, yellow lines, pedestrian crossing.*

Each of the photocopiable worksheets for this unit requires the children to have looked at the parking arrangements on the school premises and to have considered the need for safety. They should have discussed what is meant by a busy or quiet road and will need to have carried out a small-scale study about parking in the local area, with consideration being given to how to plan a fair test.

The survey should consider: where parking is provided; places where parking may cause an obstruction to others; reasons why people may want to park (for example, residents' parking, visitors' parking, deliveries) and different types of vehicle that may want to park there. Ways in which parking is controlled in the area should be looked at, and the children should be encouraged to express views about how to make an area safer.

Where in the world is Barnaby Bear®?

Unit 5

✔ **Learning outcome** (page 51)
To understand that people travel to other places.

✔✔ **Learning outcome** (page 52)
To understand the suitability of different types of transport in relation to travelling to different places.

✔✔✔ **Learning outcome** (page 53)
To plan a visit for Barnaby Bear®.

This unit encourages children to learn more about other countries and places they have travelled to, through discussion and through the adventures of Barnaby Bear®. Children should become familiar with vocabulary related to travel (including *travel, passport, transport, boat, aeroplane, train, coach, country*) and different items that might be taken on holiday (*coins, clothes, sun hat, sun cream, suitcase*).

The photocopiables in this unit require the children to have talked about journeys they have made themselves and the types of transport they have used. Photocopiable page 51 asks the children to describe places that they have visited on holiday. They could go on to talk about what they would need to pack for a holiday in one of their chosen locations. Photocopiable page 52 introduces the children to Barnaby Bear® and encourages them to think about which method of transport would be appropriate for travel to different places and why. Some of the children might work on photocopiable page 53, which asks them to plan a holiday for Barnaby, thinking about what he will need to take with him and things he might do while there.

Name ______________________ Date ______________

Around our school – the local area

- Draw two buildings that you find in your local area.

- Write a sentence about a building you have drawn.

____

____

Record of Achievement

I can identify two buildings in my local area. ☐

Name ______________________________ Date ____________________

Around our school – the local area

- Draw and label four buildings that you find in your local area.

- Choose one of the buildings. Explain what it is used for.

____

____

____

____

Record of Achievement

I can identify four buildings in my local area. ☐

Name ______________________________ Date __________________

Around our school – the local area

- Draw a building in your local area.
- Write about what it is used for.

- Draw an outdoor place in your local area.
- Write about what it is used for.

- Draw something you think would improve your local area and write a sentence to explain why it would make the area better.

Record of Achievement

I can identify places in my local area and suggest an improvement. ☐

Name ______________________________ Date ____________________

How can we make our local area safer?

- Think of a delivery vehicle that comes to your school. Write its name here.

____

- Draw the vehicle parked in a dangerous place at your school.

- Draw the vehicle parked in a safe place at your school.

Record of Achievement

I can identify a safe place to park at my school. ☐

Name ______________________ Date ______________

How can we make our local area safer?

- Stick the results of your local traffic survey here.

- What did you find out about your local traffic?

____

____

- Look at the picture below. Put a ring round the things you think would make the road near your school safer.

Record of Achievement *I can carry out a local traffic survey and identify ways of making the road safer.* ☐

Name ______________________ Date ______________

How can we make our local area safer?

- Using the results of your local traffic survey, draw and label four things that could make the area outside your school or home safer for the people who live there.

- Choose one of the things and describe how it would make a difference to road safety in your area.

____

____

Record of Achievement

I can use the results of a local traffic survey to identify ways of making the road safer. ☐

Name ______________________________ Date __________________

Where in the world is Barnaby Bear®?

- Write a word to describe the weather in each of these pictures.

______________________ ______________________

- Draw a picture of a place you have travelled to.

- Write a sentence describing what the weather was like when you went there.

____

____

Record of Achievement

I understand that people travel to other places. ☐

Name ______________________ Date ______________

Where in the world is Barnaby Bear®?

- Draw three different types of transport that Barnaby Bear could use to visit different places in the UK.

- Barnaby is going to visit a country far away. How could he get there?
- Colour the **most suitable** method of transport in **green**.
- Colour the **least suitable** method of transport in **red**.

- Why have you chosen these methods of transport?

____

____

Record of Achievement

I can identify types of transport and recognise that some types of transport are more suitable than others. ☐

Name ______________________ Date ______________

Where in the world is Barnaby Bear®?

- Barnaby Bear wants to visit a sunny country far away. If you were a travel agent, which country would you suggest Barnaby went to?

____

- What will Barnaby Bear need to take with him when he visits a sunny country far away?

____

- How do you think he will travel there?

____

- Where will he stay?

____

- Draw two activities he could do on his holiday.

Record of Achievement

I can plan a visit for Barnaby Bear. ☐

ICT

Information communications technology gives children the opportunity to develop their computer skills across all of the curriculum, as well as in dedicated ICT time. The QCA Scheme of Work for ICT states that *It should however be recognised that not all ICT learning will involve the use of a computer,* and so children should spend time developing their knowledge and understanding of information and how to select and prepare it, as well as developing their skills in using hardware and software to manipulate information in problem solving, recording and expressive work. In Year 1, children cover work on modelling, simple word-processing, labelling and classifying, representing information graphically, researching information in different ways, and following instructions.

Many of the worksheets in this section assume that practical work is done on the computer; the sheets are intended to act as a record of children's acquisition and development of the skills associated with ICT.

An introduction to modelling

Unit 1A

✔ Learning outcome (page 59)
To create, with help, a picture that represents a real or a fantasy situation.

✔✔ Learning outcome (page 60)
To create a simple representation of a real or a fantasy situation.

✔✔✔ Learning outcome (page 61)
To identify similarities and differences between a real world and a fantasy world.

This unit asks children to use ICT to organise pictures and words to create representations of real and fantasy situations on the computer. They should be introduced to the idea of a 'model' as a computer-based representation of a situation that is similar to the original, but does not replicate it exactly. Children should also begin to learn how to use the mouse to make selections on the screen and to organise information by 'clicking and dragging'. You will need access to a simple object-based drawing package (*Microsoft Office* provides a set of AutoShapes that are more than adequate) and a simple painting program (for example, *Microsoft Paint*) to create the pictures.

The photocopiables in this activity assume the children have access to computer programs that allow them to assemble pictures by clicking on items on screen or by dragging items to the correct place. Photocopiable page 59 provides a set of ideas to help children create a fantasy world. Pages 60 and 61 help the children to compare the fantasy worlds they create with the real world. It will help if they have had the opportunity to play adventure games and to have discussed in detail how people and objects in computer adventure games and simulations do not react in the same way as in real life (for example, the boy running across the field in the game will never get tired, need to stop for food or to rest). They should have had the opportunity to talk about the decisions and choices available to a player in a computer generated game and how these choices can affect the outcome of the game.

Using a word bank

Unit 1B

✔ Learning outcome (page 62)
To be able to type your name and print it out.

✔✔ Learning outcomes (page 63)
To enter words using a computer keyboard. To order sentences.

✔✔✔ Learning outcome (page 64)
To use a computer to create a sentence.

This unit introduces children to a word processor, and shows how a computer can be used to type in and assemble text on the computer screen. It provides an opportunity for children to gain experience in using the keyboard. You will need access to software that can use a word bank to present information.

When introducing children to word processing, make sure they are familiar with the layout of a computer keyboard and can name all the special keys (SPACE BAR, ENTER, DELETE).

Each of the worksheets in this activity assumes that children have already worked at the computer, and that they have developed a familiarity with the keyboard, identifying letters in both upper and lower case. They should understand that text can be entered into a computer and printed out. Photocopiable page 62 asks the children to locate the letters of their name on the keyboard; page 63 also introduces the idea of a using a word bank to make a sentence, and page 64 extends this to longer sentences created without a word bank. When the children are asked to glue their printout onto the worksheet, it is assumed that they will have been asked to use a suitable font at an acceptable size. (Children need to be able to see the text clearly on the screen, and it should fit on the sheet; 18–24 point text would be ideal.)

The information around us

Unit 1C

✔ **Learning outcome** (page 65)
To identify things that give us information through sound, pictures and text.

✔✔ **Learning outcome** (page 66)
To recognise that sounds, pictures and text convey information.

✔✔✔ **Learning outcome** (page 67)
To recognise that there are different ways of getting information.

This unit teaches children that information exists in a variety of forms, and that ICT can be used to manipulate this information. They should have the chance to experience examples of different information sources, including multimedia software such as a talking book or an adventure game.

When working on this unit, make sure that the children have become familiar with vocabulary that will allow them to identify and describe different information sources (*button, icon, information, text, graphics*).

The worksheets in this activity ask the children to identify and think about various ways in which information can be presented. Before completing the worksheets, talk about different sources of information and how they communicate to us, for example: *maps show us where things are; the sound of a television theme tune tells us the programme is about to*

begin; traffic lights tell us when to stop. Photocopiable page 65 asks children to identify the ways in which different items provide information. Pages 66 and 67 introduce the idea that some things can deliver information in more than one way, and asks children to identify these sources of information as either sound, picture or writing.

Labelling and classifying

Unit 1D

✔ **Learning outcome** (page 68)
To describe an object.

✔✔ **Learning outcome** (page 69)
To use key words to describe an object.

✔✔✔ **Learning outcome** (page 70)
To label and classify objects.

In this unit, children will learn that objects can be described and grouped according to their defining characteristics. They should be able to understand and select key words based on an object's properties, and should have experience of identifying objects by key words and of using a word processor with a word bank to present information.

Photocopiable page 68 encourages children to describe a small set of objects based on their observable characteristics (for example, *The teddy I coloured is blue; The teddy I coloured is the biggest one; The teddy I coloured has brown eyes*, and so on). Photocopiable page 69 introduces the idea of using key words to describe an object, and photocopiable page 70 asks the children to classify a set of objects according to given key words. These worksheets require the children to have had experience of object-based software with a graphic capability, and a word bank describing shapes, sizes and colours.

Representing information graphically: pictograms

Unit 1E

✔ **Learning outcome** (page 71)
To understand that ICT can be used to create a pictogram.

✔✔ **Learning outcome** (page 72)
To create a pictogram and use the data to answer questions.

✔✔✔ **Learning outcome** (page 73)
To create a pictogram and make comparisons.

This unit teaches children how to use ICT to create a pictogram to present information graphically. Children should be able to use a computer graphing package to enter data and to create their pictogram, choosing appropriate symbols. They should be able to use the data in their pictograms to answer simple questions and make comparisons.

Children will need to be familiar with vocabulary related to collecting data and creating graphs (*pictogram, icons, collect, sort, classify*).

The photocopiables in this activity assume that the children have completed a survey and have collected pictures of modes of transport to make pictograms showing how they travel to school. Using a graphing package of your choice, the children need to be shown how to enter data into the program and how icons can be used to represent the data. Photocopiable page 71 asks children to extract simple information from the pictogram provided; they need to understand that pictograms show information at a glance. Photocopiable page 72 also asks the children to create their own pictogram based on a similar survey, and photocopiable page 73 requires the children to make their own pictogram and use it to make comparisons from the data they present.

Understanding instructions and making things happen

Unit 1F

✔ **Learning outcome** (page 74)
To understand that sequencing affects outcome.

✔✔ **Learning outcomes** (page 75)
To order a set of instructions. To predict the outcome of a set of instructions.

✔✔✔ **Learning outcomes** (page 76)
To order and predict the outcome of a set of instructions. To produce an accurate set of instructions.

This unit teaches the children how to give and follow instructions in order to make things happen. They should know how to put a set of instructions into order, so that others can follow them and predict accurately what the outcome will be.

When working through this unit, children will need to be familiar with the vocabulary of instructions (*sequence, order, instruction*), and specific vocabulary pertaining to a set of instructions (*video, tape recorder, stop, start, rewind, fast forward, record*).

Before completing the worksheets, children will need to understand that machines follow instructions, and must be switched on, switched off and controlled. They should have had experience of identifying machines with on/off switches and realise that they can be controlled by a sequence of physical actions. Using a tape recorder in the classroom to record their voices is a good way of illustrating this point, and shows the need for accuracy when giving instructions. PE lessons can be used to reinforce directional language and help the children gain experience in following detailed instructions. Photocopiable page 74 asks children to sequence pictures to put a set of instructions in the correct order. It is also important that they recognise the importance of precision in instructions – ask children to look at the jumbled-up instructions on photocopiable page 75 and to think about what would happen if the instructions were carried out in the wrong order. They should have had practice in writing instructions for other members of the class to carry out – photocopiable page 76 requires the children to think about this and to write instructions in the correct order.

Name ______________________________ Date ____________________

An introduction to modelling

- In the space below, stick a printout of the picture you created on the computer using software chosen by your teacher. Make sure your picture includes a house, a tree, a vehicle and a person.

Record of Achievement *I can with help create a simple representation on the computer.* ☐

Name ______________________ Date ______________

An introduction to modelling

- Stick a printout of the picture you created on the computer in the space below.

- Write a sentence to say how your model is different from the real world.

____

____

Record of Achievement

I can explain how my representation is different from the real world. ☐

Name ______________________ Date ______________

An introduction to modelling

- Stick a printout of the picture you created on the computer in the space below.

- Explain the difference between computer game situations and the real world.

____

____

____

Record of Achievement

I can create a representation on the computer and identify similarities and differences between real or fantasy situations. ☐

Name ______________________ Date ______________

Using a word bank

- Write the letters of your first name in the boxes above the keyboard. Use one box for each letter.
- Write the letters of your surname in the boxes underneath the keyboard. Use one box for each letter.

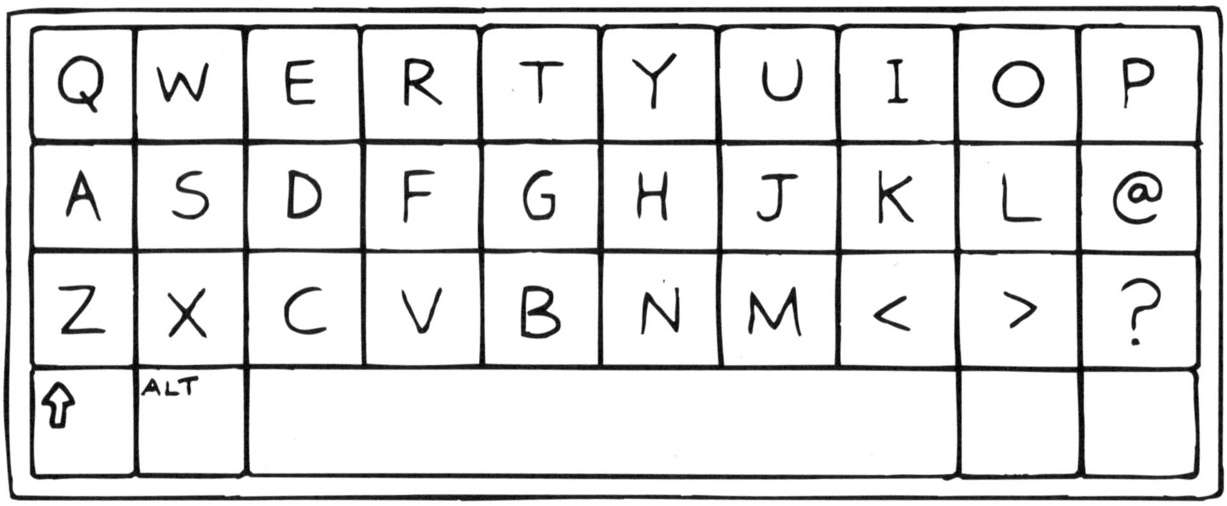

- Match each letter in your name to the correct key on the keyboard.
- Use the computer keyboard to type your name on the screen. Print out your work, then cut it out and stick it in the box below.

Record of Achievement

I can type my name. ☐

Name ______________________ Date ______________

Using a word bank

- Write the letters of your first name in the boxes above the keyboard. Use one box for each letter.
- Write the letters of your surname in the boxes underneath the keyboard. Use one box for each letter.

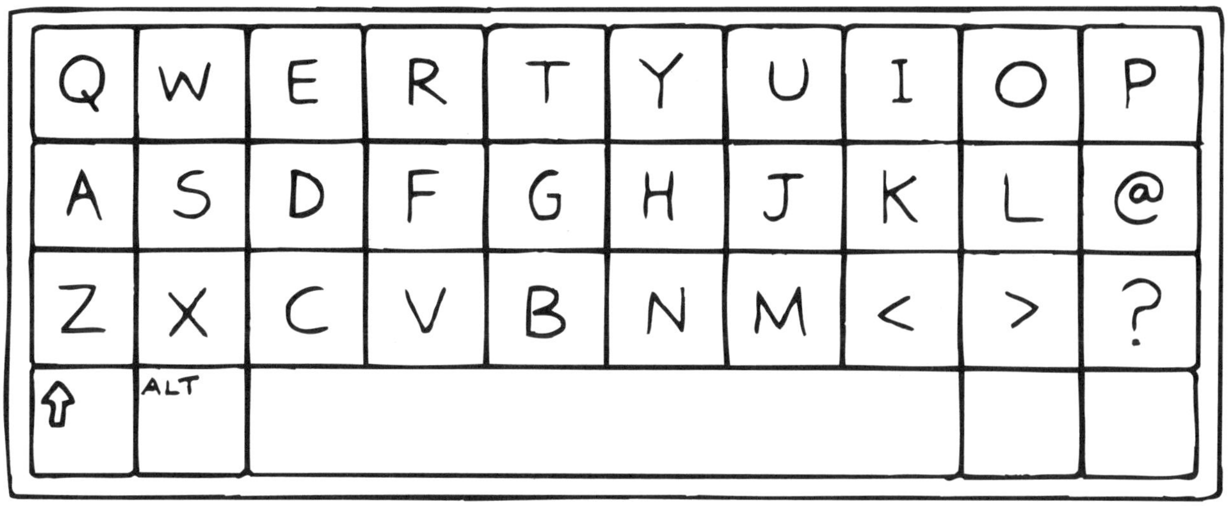

- Match each letter to the correct key on the keyboard.
- The words in this sentence are jumbled up. Write them in the correct order on the line below.

cat	The	is	the	on	mat.

____

- Use the keyboard to type your name on the screen.
- Now copy the sentence you unjumbled under your name.
- Print out your work.

Record of Achievement

I can type my name and a sentence. ☐

Name ______________________ Date ______________

Using a word bank

- Write your full name in the box below.

- Colour in red the keys you would use to spell your name on the keyboard.

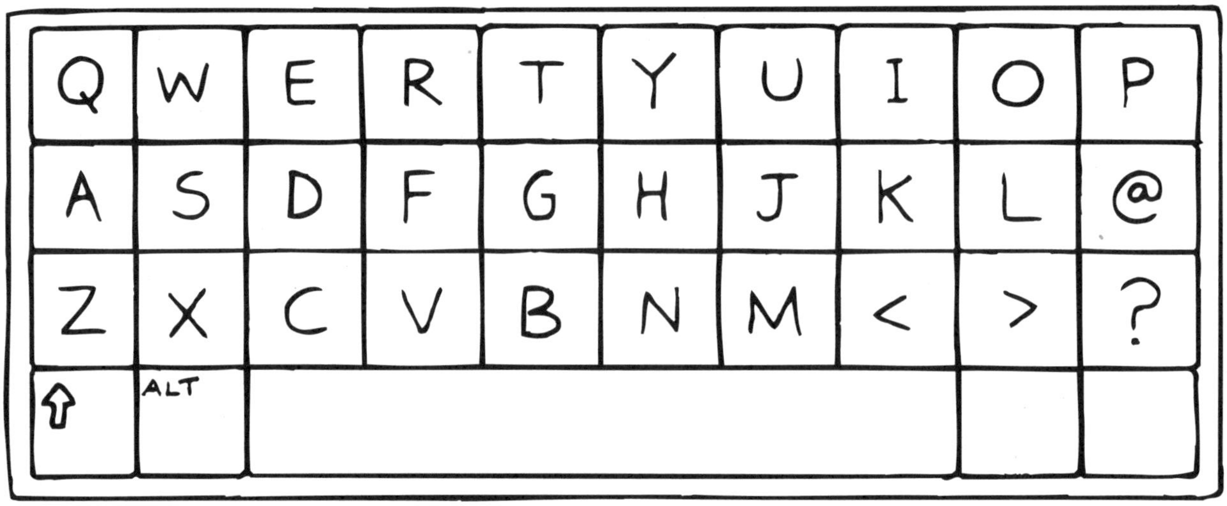

- Write a sentence about yourself in the box below.

- Using the computer keyboard, type your name on screen.
- Now type the sentence you wrote under your name.
- Print out your work, then cut it out and stick it in the box below.

Record of Achievement

I can type a sentence that I have written. ☐

Name ______________________ Date ______________

The information around us

- Which objects give you information by making a sound? Colour them in.

- Which objects give you information in pictures? Colour them in.

- Which objects give you information in writing? Colour them in.

- Which object can use sound, pictures and text to give you information?

____

- Name another object in your house that uses all three ways to give you information.

____

Record of Achievement

I can recognise different ways of getting information. ☐

Name ______________________________ Date ____________________

The information around us

- Look at the objects below and decide how they give you information.
- Do they use **sound**, **pictures** or **writing**? Some use all three ways!
- Draw lines to match each picture to the correct word or words.

sound
pictures
text

- Which objects can use all three ways to give you information?

____

____

Record of Achievement

I can recognise different ways of getting information. ☐

Name ______________________________ Date ____________________

The information around us

- Look at these objects. Decide how each object gives you information and tick the box. Some objects may have ticks in more than one box.

Object	Sound	Picture	Writing
newspaper 			
CD player 			
television 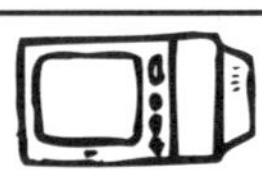			
telephone 			
bell 			
police siren 			
painting 			
letter 			
shop sign 			
picture book 			
map 			

- Which objects can use all three ways to give you information?

____

Record of Achievement

I can recognise different ways of getting information. ☐

Name ______________________ Date ______________

Labelling and classifying

- Colour each of these teddies a different colour.

- Describe one of the teddies you have coloured.

____

____

Record of Achievement

I can describe an object. ☐

Name ______________________ Date ______________

Labelling and classifying

- Colour these balls the correct colour.

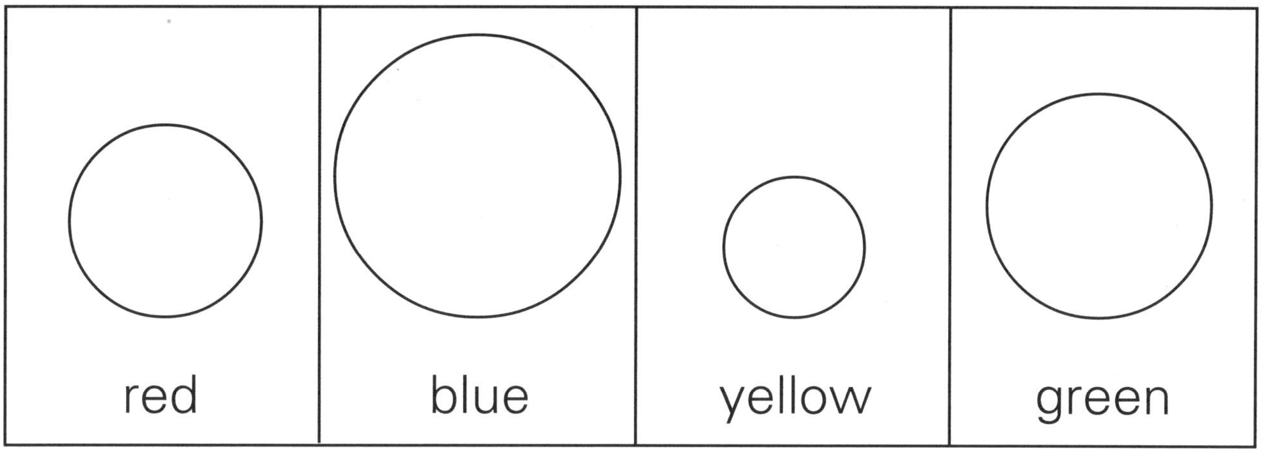

- Choose one of the balls and draw it in the box below.
- Colour the key words that describe your ball.

red	big
blue	little
yellow	round
green	square

- Write a sentence to describe your ball using the key words.

____

Record of Achievement

I can use key words to describe an object. ☐

Name ______________________________ Date ____________________

Labelling and classifying

- Colour the shapes in each group to match the key words.

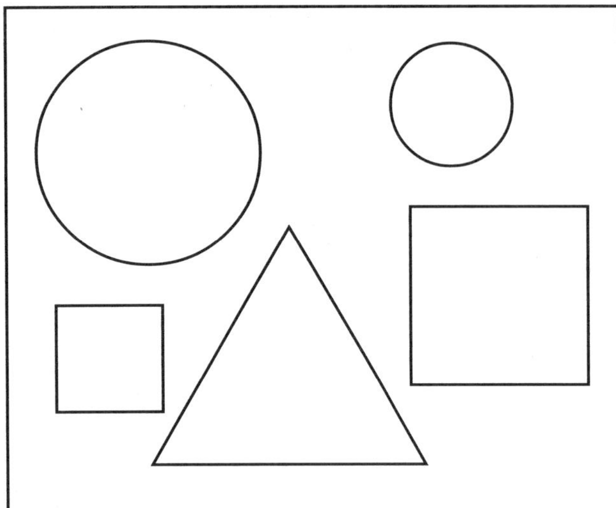	
Colour the **big** shapes in red.	Colour the **big**, **round** shapes in yellow.
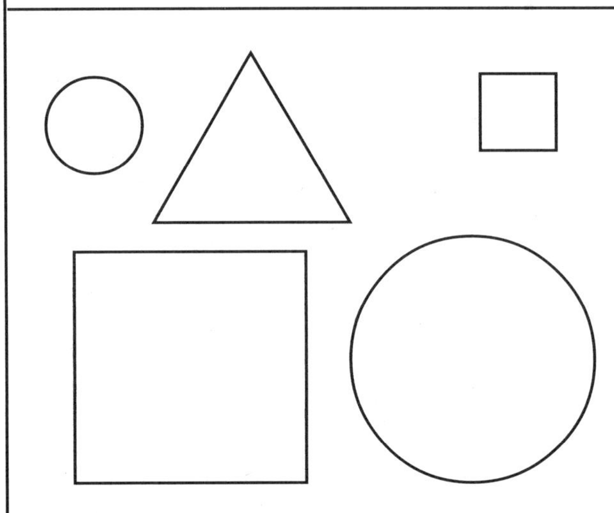	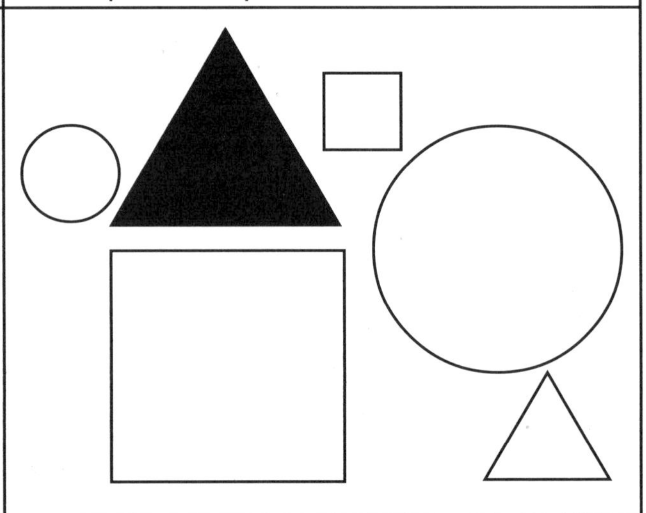
Colour the **small triangles** in green.	

- Write the key words that describe the shaded shape in the fourth box.

Record of Achievement *I can label and classify objects.* ☐

Name ______________________________ Date ____________________

Representing information graphically: pictograms

- This pictogram shows how some children at Bilton Primary School travel to school each day. Put a ring round the correct answer.

How many children walk to school each day? 1 2 3 4 5

How many children come to school in a car? 1 2 3 4 5

How many children come to school on a bike? 1 2 3 4 5

How many children come to school on a scooter? 1 2 3 4 5

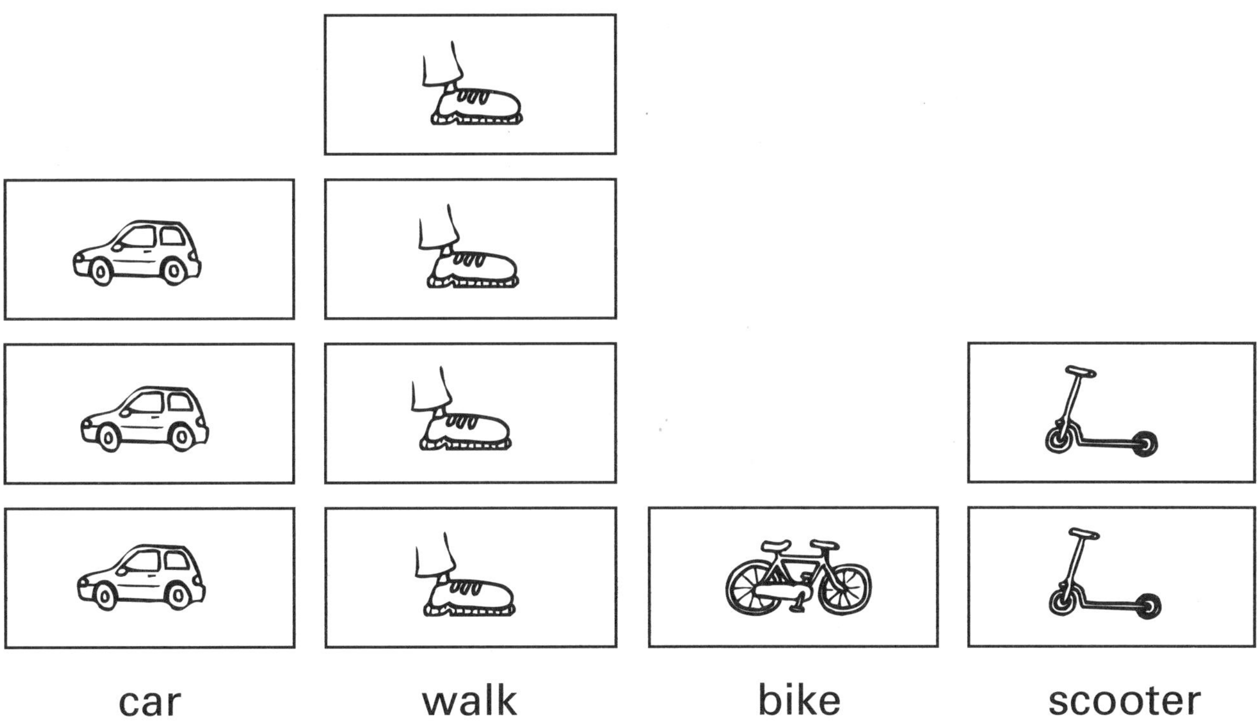

Record of Achievement

I can use a pictogram to answer simple questions. ☐

Name ______________________________ Date ________________

Representing information graphically: pictograms

This pictogram shows how some children at Bilton Primary School travel to school each day.

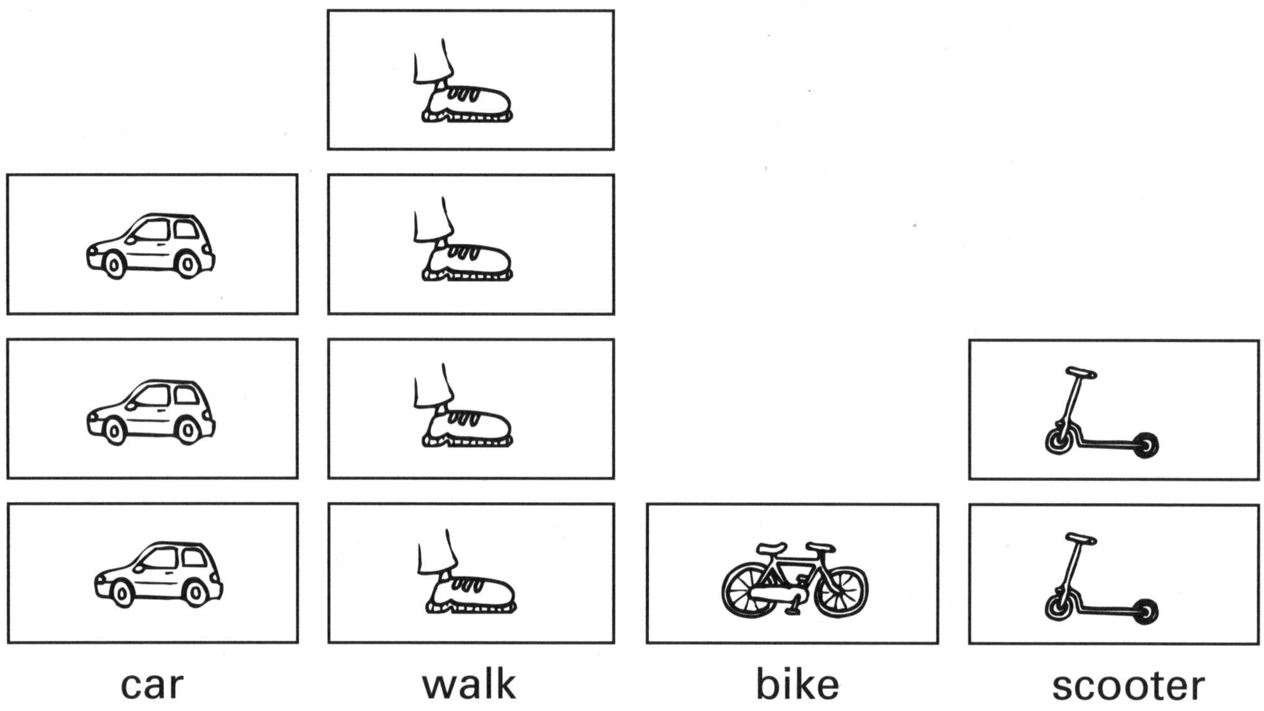

How many children walk to school each day? __________

How many children come to school in a car? __________

How many children come to school on a bike? __________

What is the most popular way to travel to school? ________

What is the least favourite way to travel? __________

- Use the computer to make a pictogram showing how the children in your class travel to school.

Record of Achievement

I can use a pictogram to answer simple questions and create a pictogram on the computer. ☐

Name ______________________________ Date ____________________

Representing information graphically: pictograms

● In the space below, draw a pictogram using this information about how a group of children at Bilton Primary School travel to school each day.

5 children travelled by car	3 children travelled by bus
6 children travelled on foot	2 children travelled by scooter
1 child used the bus	

● Answer these questions based on your pictogram. Remember to answer in a sentence.

Which was the most popular way to travel to school?

____

How many more children travelled by car than by scooter?

____

Record of Achievement

I can make a pictogram and answer questions about it. ☐

Name ______________________ Date ______________

Understanding instructions and making things happen

- Look carefully at the pictures below. Number them in the correct order so that someone following them would be able to put a tape into a video and watch a film they wanted to see.

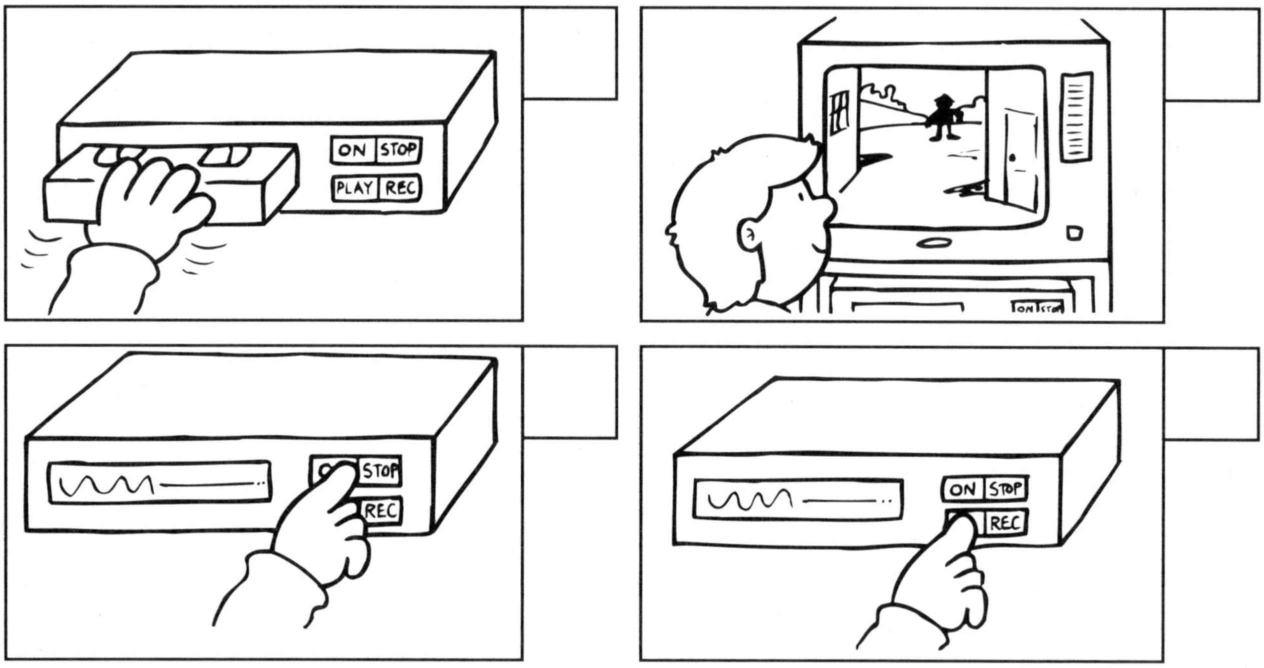

- Look at the pictures below. What would happen if you followed the instructions in them?

____

Record of Achievement

I can sequence pictures to show how to play a video. ☐

Name ______________________ Date ______________

Understanding instructions and making things happen

● These jumbled-up instructions tell you how to rewind a video tape and then watch it. Rewrite them in the correct order.

Press play on the video.
Switch on the video using the power button.
Press the rewind button.
Put the video cassette into the video.

1 ______________________

2 ______________________

3 ______________________

4 ______________________

● Once you have followed these instructions what would you be doing?

____

● Think of two reasons why you might need to rewind a video tape.

____

____

Record of Achievement

I can read a set of instructions and predict the outcome. ☐

Name ______________________________ Date ____________________

Understanding instructions and making things happen

- The jumbled-up instructions below tell you how to rewind a video tape, play the programme you want to watch and then stop the video. Rewrite them in the correct order.

Press play on the video. Press the stop button. Switch on the video using the power button. Press the rewind button. Put the video cassette into the video. Watch the programme.

1 ____

2 ____

3 ____

4 ____

5 ____

6 ____

- Write some instructions telling someone how to stop a video that is playing and place the video back in its box.

____

____

Record of Achievement

I can write an accurate set of instructions. ☐

Art and design

Art and design provides children with the opportunity to develop their creativity and imagination. In Year 1, they are able to explore the visual, tactile and sensory qualities of materials and processes, developing an understanding of how to use colour, shape and space, and pattern and texture to represent their own ideas and feelings.

Self-portrait

Unit 1A

✔ **Learning outcome** (page 80)
To communicate ideas through a self-portrait.

✔✔ **Learning outcome** (page 81)
To explore ideas based on self-portraits.

✔✔✔ **Learning outcome** (page 82)
To suggest ways to improve a piece of work.

This unit encourages children to use individual self-portraits to tell the viewer something about themselves. Before creating their own work, they should investigate images of children in drawings and look at a range of photographs and other artists' self-portraits to help them develop their own ideas – talk with them about what they see, what they like, and what they think the pictures tell them about the artist. It's useful for the children to look at a wide range of different media, including photographs, family albums, advertisements, and portraits by different artists. Look specifically at what the subjects wore and how they are different from each other.

When working on portraits, make sure that the children are familiar with words and phrases that allow them to describe images, for example for a line (*thin, bold, wavy*), colour (*bright, dull, dark*) and texture (*smooth, rough*). They will also need to experience a range of drawing materials (including soft graphite pencils, charcoal, pastels, oil pastels) and painting materials and equipment (block, powder or liquid paint, large- and small-bristled brushes).

Before working on these activities, children should pay close attention to how the artists convey ideas about themselves. For example, how might they show great wealth? (Possibly through the clothes the artist is wearing in the picture.) Children should look closely at themselves and each other and talk about how they would like to be seen by others. Each of the photocopiable activities asks the children to draw a self-portrait in the space on the page. At all times they must be encouraged to review what they have done. Photocopiable page 80 asks children to choose part of their picture that they particularly like; page 81 asks them to offer suggestions as to how they could improve their work in the future. Encourage children to look at other artists' work with a critical eye when completing photocopiable page 82.

Investigating materials

Unit 1B

✔ **Learning outcomes** (page 83)
To make a weaving from different materials. To form ideas about their work.

✔✔ **Learning outcomes** (page 84)
To make a weaving from different materials. To communicate ideas about a piece of work.

✔✔✔ **Learning outcomes** (page 85)
To make a sculpture. To describe their work and consider ways of improving it.

This unit introduces children to the different qualities of materials, both natural and manufactured, through learning the skill of weaving. It should help them to develop an understanding of colour and texture, and of how materials are used in everyday situations. They should experience working with a wide range of fabrics, natural materials (*twigs, leaves, feathers*) and manufactured materials (*straws, plastics, foil, string*).

Children should be familiar with the vocabulary to describe different materials (*natural, manufactured, textiles, velvet, lace, satin*), their visual qualities (in terms of *colour, texture*) and their tactile qualities (*flexible, soft, smooth*).

The worksheets in this unit require the children to have investigated weaving, working on either ready-made looms or ones made from boxes or paper plates. Photocopiable page 83 asks the children to describe their work and what they think about it. When weaving, encourage the children to choose their materials to communicate ideas and meanings (such as contrasting textures, or everyday materials), giving reasons for their choice. Encourage the children to think about which is their favourite material to weave with and why – photocopiable page 84 encourages them to clarify their thoughts on this. Provide opportunities for the children to think about how they would like to improve their work in the future, for example *That would have looked better if I had done it in green*, or *I should have used this fabric as it would have been more flexible and easier to weave with.* They can record their thoughts on photocopiable page 85.

What is sculpture?

Unit 1C

✔ **Learning outcome** (page 86)
To give a personal opinion about a piece of art.

✔✔ **Learning outcome** (page 87)
To think about the 'meaning' of a three-dimensional form.

✔✔✔ **Learning outcomes** (page 88)
To look at texture. To think of ways of improving a piece of work.

Children will develop their understanding of shape, form and texture in this unit through looking at the work of a variety of sculptors such as Henry Moore, Alexander Calder, Pablo Picasso and Andy Goldsworthy. Look at different kinds of sculpture through photographs and, if possible, organise visits to any work in the local area.

Make sure that the children can use vocabulary to describe sculpture, including words such as *natural materials, made materials, reclaimed materials, carving, modelling, constructing.*

The worksheets in this unit require the children to have identified the materials used in sculpture and to have made comments about different pieces of work, showing a basic understanding of why materials were chosen. They should have had experience of creating their own sculpture based on their favourite place, and should be able to talk about what it means to them – look at different ways of joining parts of the sculpture if necessary. Photocopiable page 86 encourages them to think about what the sculpture represents; pages 87 and 88 extend this by asking them to think about their choice of material (for example, textures representing the different features the sculpture portrays: hair – rough, skin – smooth), and how they might improve the sculpture.

Name ____________________ Date ______________

Self-portrait

- Draw a picture of your face. Use a mirror to help you.

- What do you like about your drawing?

____

____

____

Record of Achievement

I can draw a self-portrait. ☐

Name ______________________ Date ______________

Self-portrait

- Draw a self-portrait in the space below, showing your ideas about yourself.

- How would you like to improve your work?

____

____

____

Record of Achievement

I can improve and adapt my work. ☐

Name ______________________ Date ______________

Self-portrait

- Make a copy of another artist's self-portrait that you have looked at in class.

- The artist is ______________________

- Describe the self-portrait you looked at.

____

____

____

Record of Achievement

I can explore ideas about self-portraits.

☐

Name ________________________ Date ________________

Investigating materials

- Draw a picture of your weaving in the box below.

- Write a sentence about your weaving.

____

____

____

Record of Achievement

I can weave. ☐

Name ______________________ Date ______________

Investigating materials

- Draw a picture of your weaving in the box below.
- Make a list of the materials you used in your weaving.

Materials

- Put a tick next to the material you liked best.
- Why did you choose this material?

____

____

____

Record of Achievement

I can communicate ideas about my weaving. ☐

Name ______________________ Date ______________

Investigating materials

- Draw a picture of your weaving in the box below.

- Write about what you liked and found interesting about the texture and colour you used in your weaving.

____

____

____

- How could you improve or adapt your work?

____

____

Record of Achievement

I can explore and communicate ideas about my weaving. ☐

Name ______________________ Date ______________

What is sculpture?

- Draw a picture or stick a photograph of a sculpture you have made or seen in the box.

- What do you like best about the sculpture?

____

____

Record of Achievement

I can identify things I like about my own or others work. ☐

Name ______________________________ Date ____________________

What is sculpture?

- Draw a picture or stick a photograph of a sculpture you have made or seen in the box.

- Name the material it is made from.

____

- Write a sentence about it.

____

____

- How would you like to improve the sculpture?

____

____

Record of Achievement *I can explore ideas and communicate meanings in three-dimensional form.* ☐

Name ______________________ Date ______________

What is sculpture?

- Draw a picture or stick a photograph of a sculpture you have made in the space below.

- Describe how the sculpture feels when you touch it.

____

____

- What would you do to improve the sculpture?

____

____

Record of Achievement *I can identify things I would like to improve in my work.* ☐

Music

Music provides the opportunity for children to make and respond to sound, developing their understanding and appreciation of a wide range of different kinds of music. With each of these units, children acquire the knowledge, skills and understanding needed to make music. They develop the interrelated skills of composing, performing and appraising. In Year 1, children concentrate on making sounds of varying lengths, recognising different sounds and using instruments to make and perform different sounds. Due to the practical nature of studying music, not all of the QCA's outcomes are covered in this chapter.

Sounds interesting: exploring sounds

Unit 2

✔ **Learning outcome** (page 91)
To recognise how different sounds are made.

✔✔ **Learning outcome** (page 92)
To make and change different sounds.

✔✔✔ **Learning outcome** (page 93)
To use instruments to represent different sounds.

In following this unit the children should develop the ability to identify different sounds and be able to use sounds expressively. Encourage the children to use a variety of equipment, including their own bodies, to experiment with making and changing sounds; help them to choose sounds that reflect the mood of other pieces of music. You might like to create a class performance, using sound to enhance the telling of a story.

These activities require the children to become familiar with vocabulary related to playing instruments (*pluck, strum, blow, hit*). They should be able to describe the sounds they hear in terms of dynamics (*loud, quiet*), tempo, (*fast, slow*), pitch (*high, low*) and timbre (*rattling, banging, scraping*), and be able to describe changes in sounds qualitatively (*louder, quieter, faster, slower*).

The worksheets in this unit assume that the children have had the opportunity to make a variety of sounds using their voices and a selection of found objects and instruments. They should have heard and identified different sounds and begun to explore classroom instruments. Photocopiable page 91 requires the children to explore how these instruments make a sound. When completing photocopiable page 92, encourage the children to use their knowledge of sounds to think about how they could change them to reflect the mood of chants and songs. Photocopiable page 93 extends this, asking the children to think about the qualities of different sounds and what these might be for. The children's work could contribute to the development of a class performance.

The long and the short of it

Unit 3

✔ **Learning outcome** (page 94)
To make sounds of varying lengths using musical instruments.

✔✔ **Learning outcome** (page 95)
To create a sequence of long and short sounds.

✔✔✔ **Learning outcome** (page 96)
To compose and perform a sequence of long and short sounds.

This unit asks children to develop their understanding of long and short sounds, and to put together an interesting sequence of sound.

Children will need to develop their use of vocabulary to describe different sounds, especially in terms of duration (*long, short*).

The worksheets for this unit assume that children have explored vocal and instrumental sounds, and that they have had the opportunity to play percussion instruments, organising their sounds with a steady pulse. To complete the worksheets, children need to have access to a selection of instruments on which they can play sounds of varying lengths. Photocopiable page 94 focuses on identifying instruments that make long and short sounds. Talk to the children and help them use this knowledge to create a sequence of sounds. Photocopiable pages 95 and 96 ask the children to create and perform sequences of sounds, which will need to be recorded on the sheet. It's up to you and the children to decide how to record the notation; you could decide together what symbols to use.

Name ______________________________ Date ____________________

Sounds interesting: exploring sounds

- How can you make a sound using these instruments? Tick the right box.

Instrument	Strum/ pluck	Blow	Hit
Guitar 	☐	☐	☐
Drum 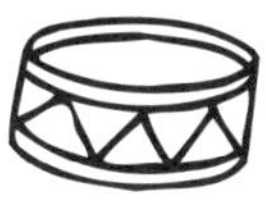	☐	☐	☐
Recorder 	☐	☐	☐
Triangle 	☐	☐	☐
Pan Pipes 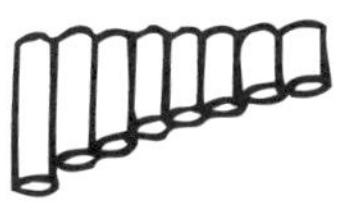	☐	☐	☐
Glockenspiel 	☐	☐	☐
Clarinet 	☐	☐	☐

Record of Achievement

I can make sounds using different instruments. ☐

Name ______________________ Date ______________

Sounds interesting: exploring sounds

- Look at these instruments.

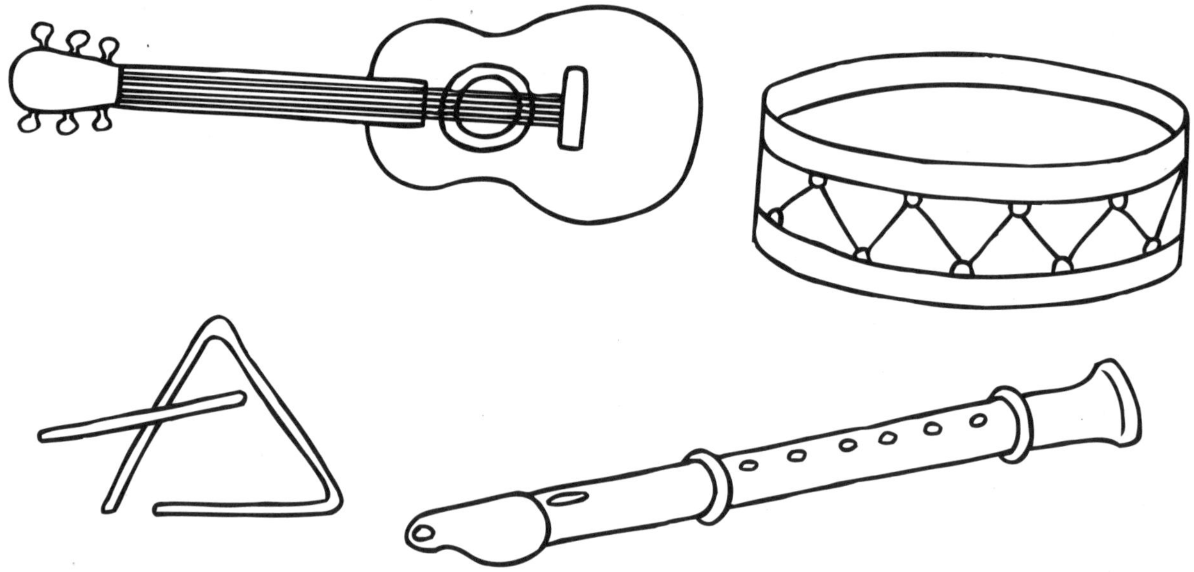

I can make the drum louder by ______________________

____

I can make the recorder louder by ______________________

____

I can make the triangle make a quiet sound by ______________

____

I can make the guitar play quiet sounds by ______________

____

Record of Achievement

I can change the sounds that different instruments make. ☐

Name ________________________ Date ______________

Sounds interesting: exploring sounds

- Play these instruments and see how many different sounds you can make with them.

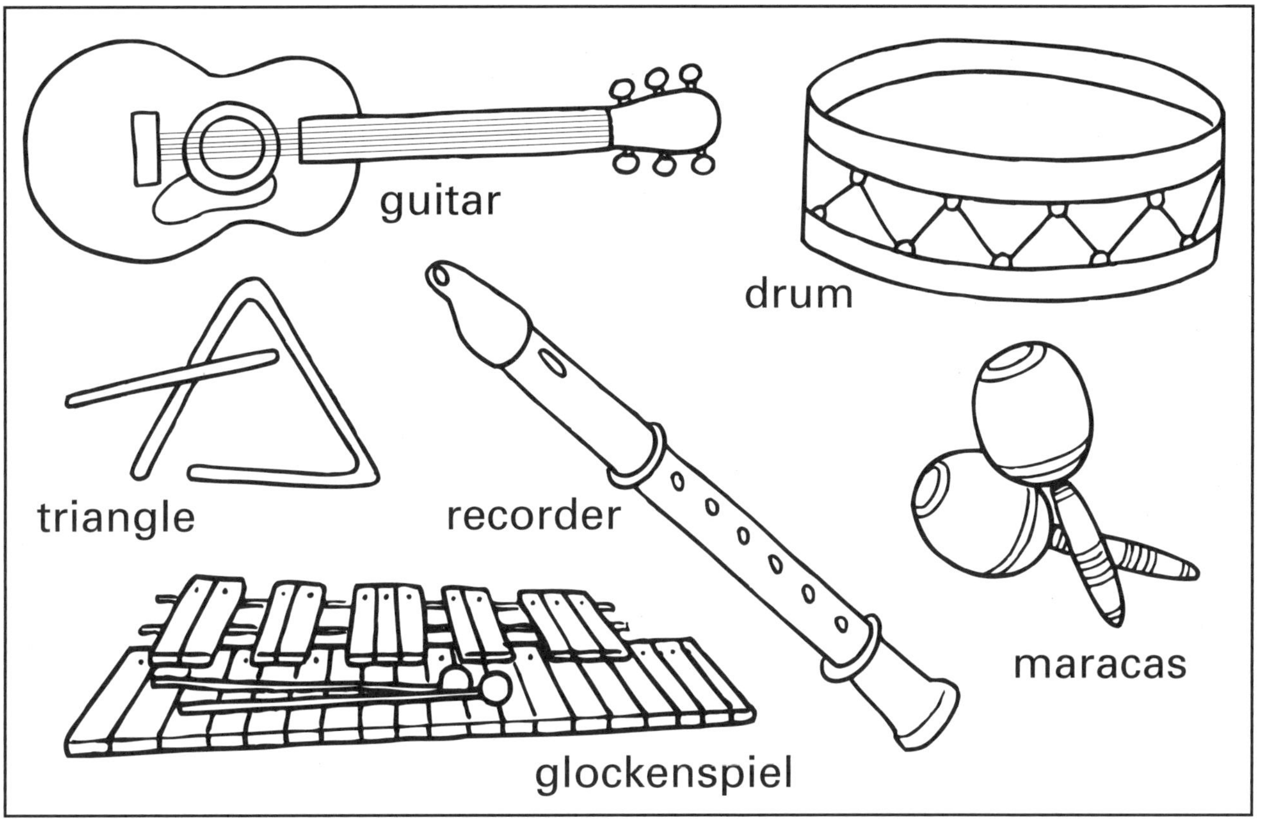

- Which instrument would you use to make a rattly sound?

____

- Which instrument would you use to make a banging sound?

____

- Which instrument would you use to make a scraping sound?

____

Record of Achievement

I can choose an instrument to make a certain sound. ☐

Name ______________________________ Date ___________________

The long and the short of it

- Choose one of the instruments below and show your teacher how to make a long sound on it.
- Choose a different instrument and show how to make a short sound on it.

- Colour in **red** the instrument you used to make a **long** sound.
- Colour in **blue** the instrument you used to make a **short** sound.
- Draw yourself playing the instrument.

Record of Achievement *I can make long and short sounds using musical instruments.* ☐

Name ______________________ Date ______________

The long and the short of it

- Choose two instruments and draw them in the boxes below.

I used this instrument to make long sounds.	I used this instrument to make short sounds.

- Work with a friend to make a sequence of long and short sounds.
- Record your sequence using symbols or pictures in the boxes below.

- Play your sequence to your teacher.

Record of Achievement *I can create a sequence of long and short sounds using musical instruments.* ☐

Name ______________________ Date ______________

The long and the short of it

- Draw and label the instruments your group are going to play in the box below.

- Compose a sequence of long and short sounds using your chosen instruments.
- Record your sequence in the boxes below using symbols to represent the sounds.

- Perform your group's sequence for your teacher.

Record of Achievement *I can compose and perform a sequence involving sounds of varying lengths.* ☐

Design and technology

Design and technology provides children with the opportunity to apply their knowledge and understanding in order to make creative and innovative products for a variety of defined purposes. Children should begin to think about and apply knowledge and understanding of: materials and components, mechanisms and control systems, structures, existing products, quality, and health and safety. They should have the opportunity to generate ideas and develop their practical skills, including those in science, maths, ICT and art.

In Year 1, children focus on mechanisms, structures and food. They have the opportunity to make moving pictures using sheet materials, make model playground equipment using construction kits, and consider healthy eating through making a fruit salad.

Moving pictures (focus – mechanisms)

Unit 1A

✔ **Learning outcome** (page 101)
To develop ideas through making.

✔✔ **Learning outcome** (page 102)
To incorporate a simple slider or lever mechanism into a moving picture.

✔✔✔ **Learning outcome** (page 103)
To evaluate a product.

This unit asks children to make a moving picture that incorporates a basic lever or slider mechanism. They should develop their understanding of movement and simple mechanisms by looking at everyday products that use levers and sliders. Encourage the children to work out how such mechanisms work, and to describe this through drawing and labelling simple diagrams. You might like to incorporate this work into a project on greetings cards or making a class book with moving pictures. Ask the children to think critically about their work, and to suggest simple reasons stating how it could be improved. Make sure that children are closely supervised at all times when using craft tools, and that they know how to use them safely.

Encourage the children to describe their work as they progress, using appropriate vocabulary to describe their designs (*idea, choose, draw, label*) and to describe their mechanism (*move, handle, lever, slider, join*). How do they think their work can be improved? (They should be familiar with words such as *better* and *improve.*)

The worksheets in this activity require the children to have looked at examples of simple levers and sliding mechanisms in books, cards and other products that have moving parts. They should have made, described and discussed a moving picture of some kind over the previous weeks. It is important that the children can describe how a lever or slider works in a mechanism, and that they have considered improvements to their own design, for example *The lever is a bit limp, but I could use thicker card to strengthen it.* Photocopiable pages 101 and 102 encourage the children to think about how their mechanism works; page 103 asks them to draw and label their work, and to think about how it could be improved.

Playgrounds (focus – structures)

Unit 1B

✔ **Learning outcome** (page 104)
To use materials to make a model.

✔✔ **Learning outcomes** (page 105)
To make a model of some playground equipment. To evaluate the model.

✔✔✔ **Learning outcomes** (page 106)
To make a model of some playground equipment with a moving part. To evaluate the model.

These activities give children the opportunity to learn about structures through everyday experience of playground equipment. They should have looked at real-life playgrounds and playground equipment before making their own working models based on what they have seen. Encourage the children as they work to think about framework structures and how to make models that are stable and able to support loads. Through the making assignment, they should think about what materials are used for play equipment and how they can be assembled.

Children should be able to use appropriate vocabulary to describe their work, relating to designing, making, and knowledge and understanding (*plan, join, structure*). They should be able to describe materials (*wood, metal, plastic*), 2-D and 3-D shapes, and should be able to evaluate their work (*better, stronger, improve*).

The worksheets for this unit assume that the children have investigated and drawn pictures of real-life playground equipment (slides, swings, climbing frames) before making their own models using construction kits, sheet materials and reclaimed materials. Photocopiable page 104 asks the children to draw and label a plan of their model. They should have had the opportunity to test and discuss their products at various stages of development, for example *I need more glue on that part to make the join stronger; that piece of card needs to be longer.* It would be useful for the children to evaluate each other's work, but make sure this is done in a positive manner (*The ladder is a bit wobbly but it would be fun to use*). Pages 105 and 106 encourage the children to look at their work critically and to think about how it might be improved.

Eat more fruit and vegetables (focus – food)

Unit 1C

✔ **Learning outcome** (page 107)
To recognise and name different fruits and choose items for a product.

✔✔ **Learning outcome** (page 108)
To use sensory vocabulary to describe texture, taste and appearance.

✔✔ **Learning outcome** (page 109)
To understand the need to use tools safely.

✔✔✔ **Learning outcome** (page 110)
To consider alternative appropriate ideas and justify choices.

This unit aims to develop children's understanding of the properties of different fruits and underline the importance of a healthy diet. When working through this unit, provide children with the opportunity to taste a variety of different fruits, describing the different tastes and textures they sample – making a fruit salad is a good project for the children to work on. This unit provides an opportunity to introduce the children to the need for hygiene when handling food, and how to use basic kitchen tools safely.

When working on this unit, ensure the children have become familiar with words and phrases that describe taste and texture (such as *sharp, juicy, sweet, scented, crunchy*) and that describe food preparation (*choosing, peeling, slicing*) and safety in the kitchen.

The worksheets in this unit require the children to recognise and name a variety of different kinds of fruit; they will need to have previous knowledge of the tools used in food preparation and the need for safety in the kitchen. Encourage the children to sample fruits; photocopiable page 107 asks them to describe some fruits, and to think about possible ingredients for a fruit salad. Page 108 develops this topic, encouraging the children to think about specific qualities of different fruits, and page 109 helps the children to decide on the contents and method of preparation for a fruit salad. When making their salad, the children will need to talk about what their finished product should look like and consider changes that could be made, for example *The fruit salad is too green in appearance; next time I could add some strawberries and oranges.* Photocopiable page 110 encourages the children to think of alternative ingredients for their salad, and to think about reasons for their choices.

Homes (focus – structures)

Unit 1D

✔ **Learning outcome** (page 111)
To make a model of a home using reclaimed materials.

✔✔ **Learning outcome** (page 112)
To make a model of a home incorporating main features (windows, doors).

✔✔✔ **Learning outcome** (page 113)
To make a model of a home with interior rooms, cut-out windows and gutters.

Through observation of different types of building, this unit gives children the opportunity to develop their understanding of structures and how these can be made stronger and more stable. Children should draw on this experience and information when developing their own ideas, so they can make their own structures from a variety of different materials, including sheet materials and construction kits.

Children should develop vocabulary relating to designing (*draw, plan, label*), making (*join, fix, plan*), and knowledge and understanding of form and structure (*strong, weak, wall, roof* and so on). They will also require some understanding of mathematical vocabulary (*square, rectangle, triangle, cuboid, side, edge*).

The worksheets in this unit require the children to have looked at pictures, photographs and books showing different types of houses. They will need access to different construction materials (plastic, card, papers and a range of suitable reclaimed materials) when constructing their models. Experience of joining materials (such as glue and masking tape) will be essential. Before making their model the children will need to have made decisions about who their home is for, and the materials they need. Talk with the children to help clarify their ideas – ask them: *How could you do this?* On completion of their work, time must be taken to allow the children to explain why they included certain features of their model to a group or the rest of the class, for example *I put the gutter on here to catch the rain coming off the roof; these curtains go either side of that window.* The photocopiable worksheets provide an opportunity for the children to record details about their models.

Name ______________________ Date ______________

Moving pictures

- Stick the moving picture you made in the box below.

- How does your picture move?

____

____

Record of Achievement

I can make a moving picture. ☐

Name ______________________________ Date ____________________

Moving pictures

- Stick the moving picture you made that has a simple lever or slider in it in the space below.

- Describe how your lever or slider works.

____

____

Record of Achievement

I can make a moving picture and describe how a lever works. ☐

Name ______________________ Date ______________

Moving pictures

- Draw a sketch of the moving picture you made.

- Draw the lever or slider you used and explain how it worked in your picture.

- How could you improve your moving part?

Record of Achievement *I can describe how a moving part works and how it could be improved.* ☐

Name ______________________________ Date ____________________

Playgrounds

You are going to make a piece of playground equipment. You will need a construction kit.

- Plan what you are going to make. Draw your plan here.

- Draw your finished model. Label your drawing.

Record of Achievement

I can use materials to make a model.

☐

Name ______________________________ Date ____________________

Playgrounds

- Draw the model of a piece of playground equipment you have made.

- List the materials you used.

- How could you have improved your model?

____

____

____

Record of Achievement *I can use materials to make a model of some playground equipment.* ☐

Name ______________________ Date ______________

Playgrounds

- Draw the model of a piece of playground equipment you have made.
- Label the drawing with the materials you have used.

- What is the best part of your model? Why do you think this?

____

____

- How could you make your model stronger?

____

Record of Achievement

I can use materials to make a model of some playground equipment with a moving part. ☐

Name ______________________ Date ______________

Eat more fruit and vegetables

- Which items might you find in a fruit salad? Colour them in.
- Choose one of the fruits and draw what you see when it is cut in half.

- Now taste the fruit. Write a sentence describing the taste of your fruit.

____

____

Record of Achievement *I can describe a fruit and choose items to put in a fruit salad.* ☐

Name ______________________ Date ______________

Eat more fruit and vegetables

- Complete a sentence for each picture describing what an apple looks like, how it feels and what it tastes like.

The apple looks ______________________

The apple feels ______________________

The apple tastes ______________________

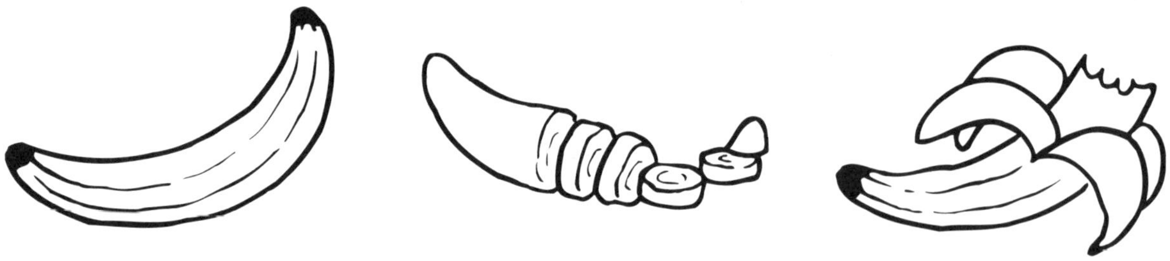

- Complete a sentence for each picture describing what a banana looks like, how it feels and what it tastes like.

The banana looks ______________________

The banana feels ______________________

The banana tastes ______________________

Record of Achievement

I can describe the properties of fruit including taste, texture and appearance. ☐

Name ______________________ Date ______________

Eat more fruit and vegetables

- List the fruit you used to make a fruit salad below.
- Write the quantity used next to the fruit.

Fruit	Quantity

- Why did you choose this mix of ingredients?

____

- Describe how you prepared yourself and the fruit for the salad.

____

- Draw a tool you used in the preparation.

- Explain how this tool could be dangerous if not used safely.

____

- Why is it important to use plenty of fruit?

____

Record of Achievement

I can prepare and combine ingredients into a specific product. ☐

Name ______________________ Date ______________

Eat more fruit and vegetables

- Plan a fruit salad for your friend which includes the following colours:

yellow, orange, green, red

and the following fruits:

apple, banana, orange, tangerine, grapes, strawberries.

- Draw and label each fruit in the bowl below.

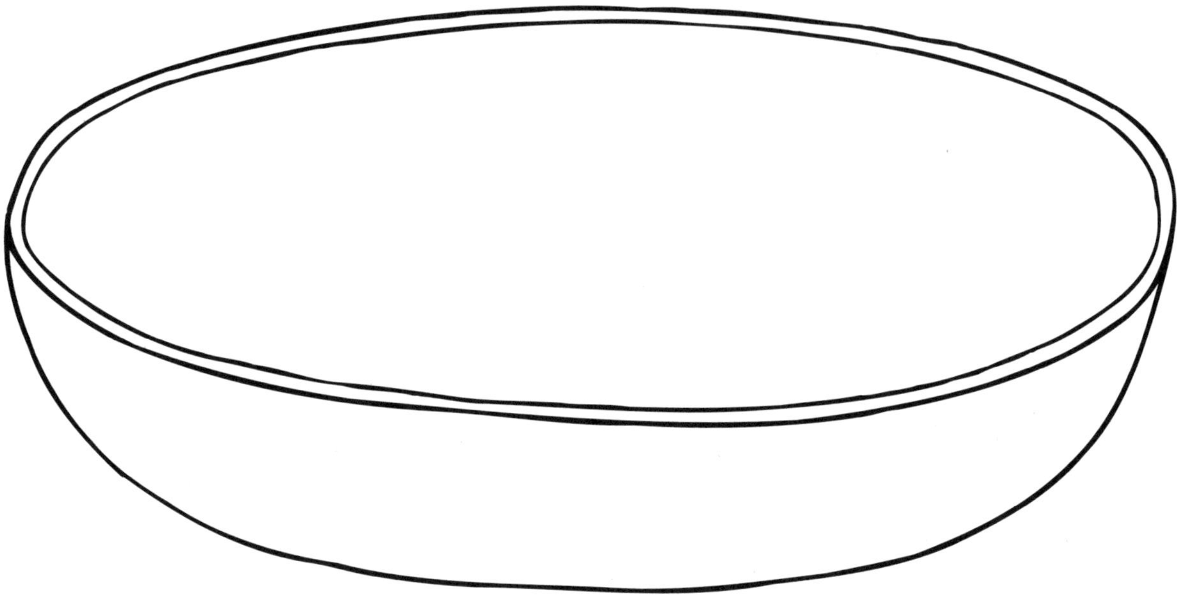

- The fruit shop has sold out of apples and grapes. Choose two other fruits to replace the apples and grapes. Write a sentence to say why you chose these fruits.

____

____

____

- Now make your fruit salad.

Record of Achievement

I can consider alternative appropriate ingredients and give reasons for my choices. ☐

Name ______________________ Date ______________

Homes

- Draw a picture of the house you made using reclaimed materials or a construction kit.

- List the materials you have used in the box below.

Record of Achievement *I can use reclaimed materials or a construction kit to make a model.* ☐

Name ______________________ Date ______________

Homes

● Draw a picture of the model home you designed and made in the space below. Label the exterior parts of your model.

My home was for ______________________

It was made from ______________________

____

It has these features: ______________________

____

Record of Achievement

I can build a model of a home and show its main features. ☐

Name ______________________ Date ______________

Homes

- Draw a picture of the model home you designed and made in the space below.

- Describe the inside of your model home, explaining why you included certain features.

____

____

____

Record of Achievement

I can build a model of a home with some interior features. ☐

Religious education

Religious education provides children with the opportunity to develop their skills in working with others and treating others with respect. It encourages them to consider their own experiences, attitudes and values, and those of other people. In listening to stories, children develop their understanding of the beliefs and cultures of others, the importance of sharing celebration and festivals, and learn about a variety of cultural and religious traditions.

In Year 1, children begin to gain an understanding of what it means to 'belong' – both to their own family and to a religious family. This work can be related to Christianity, looking at the three wise men and the giving of gifts at Christmas. Children also look in greater detail at how Jews express their beliefs, considering the celebrations of Hanukkah and Passover. Children should have had experience of visiting a local place of worship, reflecting on the atmosphere and purpose of the building.

What does it mean to belong?

Unit 1A (generic)

✔ **Learning outcome** (page 119)
To identify the idea of belonging.

✔✔ **Learning outcome** (page 120)
To understand the idea of belonging, with reference to the family.

✔✔✔ **Learning outcome** (page 121)
To understand the importance of families.

This unit explores the children's understanding of belonging to different groups and families. By relating to their own experience, they should gain a sense of what it means to belong that can be transferred to recognising how people are welcomed into different religions.

This unit introduces children to vocabulary related to religion (*God, belonging, commitment*) and to organisations that we can belong to (*school, club, Brownies, Beavers*).

The worksheets in this activity require the children to have thought about and discussed groups or societies to which they belong (the school, a football team and so on), and for them to have had access to artefacts associated with belonging (school badge, uniform and so on). Photocopiable page 119 asks children to identify something to which they belong. To complete photocopiable page 120, they should have discussed their own family life and things they do with their family, identifying ways in which they belong. For photocopiable page 121, they should have covered work that shows there are many different religions in the world and that these religions make members part of a family.

What does it mean to belong in Christianity?

Unit 1B

✔ **Learning outcome** (page 122)
To recall the main features of a baptism service.

✔✔ **Learning outcome** (page 123)
To explain the symbolism of the baptismal candle.

✔✔✔ **Learning outcome** (page 124)
To understand why Christians are baptised.

This unit extends the ideas of belonging introduced in the previous unit, and draws upon the children's own experiences and understanding of belonging to relate this to the Christian baptismal service and how this initiates a person into God's family.

Children should become familiar with words and phrases related to religion, in particular Christianity and baptism (*God, family, belonging, commitment, Jesus, baptism, christening, John the Baptist, River Jordan*).

The worksheets in this activity require the children to have had access to information and artefacts associated with a Christian baptism, such as the baptismal candle, books or videos showing a child being baptised and so on. It would also be useful if the children have visited a church to see a font for themselves, and perhaps witnessed a mock baptism. Photocopiable page 122 introduces the idea of a baptism and relates it to the idea of belonging to God's family. Children completing photocopiable page 123 should begin to understand some of the symbolism of the baptism service, in particular the baptismal candle. Photocopiable page 124 asks children to think about why children are baptised, and to understand the importance of the ceremony.

Celebrations: why do Christians give gifts at Christmas?

Unit 1C

✓ **Learning outcome** (page 125)
To name the three gifts given to Jesus by the Wise Men.

✓✓ **Learning outcome** (page 126)
To retell the main events of the visit of the Wise Men.

✓✓✓ **Learning outcome** (page 127)
To understand that Christians believe that Jesus is God's gift to the world.

✓ **Learning outcome** (page 128)
To describe personal feelings when giving or receiving gifts.

✓✓ **Learning outcome** (page 129)
To understand the concept of a precious gift.

✓✓✓ **Learning outcome** (page 130)
To describe personal feelings.

The familiar giving of gifts at Christmas provides a useful starting point for this unit of work, and introduces the idea that Christians believe that Jesus is God's gift to the world. This unit explores the familiar practice of giving gifts at Christmas; the children will have gained experience of the Christian belief that Jesus is God's gift to the world. There are two worksheets for each QCA expectation in this unit – the first three worksheets look at the giving of gifts in a Christian context, while the second set of worksheets explores more general attitudes to giving and receiving.

Children should be familiar with words and phrases related to religion, Christianity and feelings (*God, Jesus, Christmas, gift, gold, frankincense, myrrh, hope, love, joy, peace, safety, precious*).

The first set of photocopiable worksheets require the children to have looked in detail at the story of the first Christmas and the visit of the Wise Men. Photocopiable page 125 asks children to identify the three gifts that the Wise Men brought with them. Discuss the main events of the Wise Men's visit (following the star from the east, stopping at the court of King Herod, bringing gifts, returning home a different way) before children complete photocopiable page 126. Photocopiable page 127 encourages the children to think about the significance of the visit, and the idea that Jesus was God's gift to the world. Encourage them to think about the connection between God's gift, the Wise Men's gifts and the giving of gifts at Christmas.

The second set of worksheets focuses on attitudes towards giving gifts, and encourages children to think about the feelings associated with the giving of gifts. Photocopiable page 128 asks children to think about gifts they have given and received, and their feelings at the time. Encourage the children to discuss their feelings about giving and receiving gifts, for example anticipation when opening the gift, feeling grateful or pleased, and the feelings of the person who gives the gift – will they like it? Pages 129 and 130 encourage the children to make a link between the giving of gifts as part of celebrating Christmas and the feelings associated with doing so.

Beliefs and practice

Unit 1D (generic)

✔ **Learning outcome** (page 131)
To identify a key belief from a named religion.

✔✔ **Learning outcome** (page 132)
To identify a religious artefact associated with a named religion.

✔✔✔ **Learning outcome** (page 133)
To explain the symbolism of a religious artefact from a named religion.

This unit allows children to look at a faith – the choice of which is open-ended – in both a contemporary and a historical way, giving the children an opportunity to learn about current beliefs and practices, and to look at the key values of the religion being studied in order to understand their importance for those who follow the religion.

When working on this unit ensure that the children have become familiar with words and phrases related to religion you are studying.

The worksheets for this activity require that the children have access, through classroom displays or simple picture information books, to some of the religious artefacts associated with the religion you have chosen to study. Help the children to identify the artefacts and understand how and when they are used. Photocopiable page 131 asks the children to identify a key belief of the religion you are studying, and to draw an artefact. Photocopiable page 132 encourages the children to look at the religion's key beliefs and artefacts, and to think about how and why they might be used in everyday life. Children who complete photocopiable page 133 will also need a simple understanding of the symbolism associated with each artefact.

How do Jewish people express their beliefs in practice?

Unit 1E

✔ **Learning outcome** (page 134)
To retell the story of Moses' early life.

✔✔ **Learning outcome** (page 135)
To recall some key events in the life of Moses.

✔✔✔ **Learning outcome** (page 136)
To explain the importance of Moses as a great leader.

✔ **Learning outcome** (page 137)
To recognise the feast of Hanukkah.

✔✔ **Learning outcome** (page 138)
To know some key facts about the feast of Hanukkah.

✔✔✔ **Learning outcome** (page 139)
To understand the meaning of Hanukkah.

This unit provides the opportunity to learn about the historical foundation of Judaism. It outlines the religion's key beliefs and practices, and focuses on the life of Moses. There are three sets of worksheets in this unit, which aim to provide a choice between studying the life of Moses, or Hanukkah or Passover, rather than all three.

As you work through this unit, children should become familiar with words and phrases related to Jewish beliefs and practices (*Hanukkah, Passover, Shabbat, menorah, Seder meal*) and with the story of Moses.

The first set of photocopiables looks in detail at the early life of Moses, focusing on his birth, the Pharaoh's daughter finding him, and his life in the palace. Children completing photocopiable page 134 should focus on these key events of Moses' life. Time should also to be spent on explaining why Moses was thought of as a great leader and what he did for the Israelites (led them out of Egypt to the promised land). Children who complete photocopiable page 135 may like to concentrate

✔ **Learning outcome** (page 140)
To recognise the feast of Passover.

✔✔ **Learning outcome** (page 141)
To know some key facts about the feast of Passover.

✔✔✔ **Learning outcome** (page 142)
To understand the meaning of Passover.

on describing one of these events. Those who complete photocopiable page 136 should be encouraged to think about why Moses was considered a great leader, using the pictures on the worksheet to help them.

The second and third sets of worksheets concentrate on the festivals of Hanukkah and Passover. To complete photocopiable pages 137 and 140, children should recognise the important images and artefacts about Hanukkah and Passover respectively. It would be useful for children to have access to artefacts associated with these feasts that they can handle and from which they can gain first-hand experience. Photocopiable page 138 develops children's knowledge of Hanukkah, and introduces the idea of the symbolism of the menorah. Photocopiable page 139 encourages the children to think about the meaning of Hanukkah to Jews. When studying Passover, it may be appropriate to set up a table set with the Seder meal and to sample a selection of the food eaten at this feast. Photocopiable page 141 asks the children to identify key features of the Passover meal; a video showing a Jewish family celebrating these different feasts might be helpful in extending the children's knowledge. Photocopiable page 142 looks at the symbolism of the foods on the Seder plate.

What can we learn from visiting a church?

Unit 1F

✔ **Learning outcome** (page 143)
To recognise objects found in a church.

✔✔ **Learning outcome** (page 144)
To describe the use of a named object found in a church.

✔✔✔ **Learning outcome** (page 145)
To describe the atmosphere in a church.

This unit is based on a visit to a church, and is intended to extend work completed in Unit 1B. It introduces the idea that a church is a special place of worship for Christians and has a special atmosphere all of its own

When working on this unit ensure that the children have become familiar with words and phrases related to the church building and the artefacts used in the building (*altar, font, lectern, pulpit, cross, crucifix, candles*) and the atmosphere found in such a place (*calm, peaceful, dark, light*).

The worksheets in this activity assume that the children have made a visit to their local church (or if this is not possible, to have watched a video showing a range of Christian places of worship). Children should have access to some of the Christian artefacts that would be found in a church – for example, candles, a bible or hymn book, a crucifix. Photocopiable page 143 asks children to name a selection of things that are found in a church. Discuss what different things are used for in Christian worship before children complete photocopiable page 144, and ask them to think about words to describe the atmosphere inside a church before completing photocopiable page 145.

Name ______________________________ Date ____________________

What does it mean to belong?

- Draw a picture of something you belong to.

- Complete this sentence:

I belong to ____

____

Record of Achievement

I can identify something I belong to. ☐

Name ______________________________ Date ____________________

What does it mean to belong?

- Draw and label a picture of your family.

- Write about something you do with your family.

____

____

____

Record of Achievement

I understand what it's like to belong to my family. ☐

Name ______________________ Date ______________

What does it mean to belong?

- We all belong to a family. Draw and label the members of your family.

My family is special because ______________________

____

____

Belonging to a religion is special because ______________

____

____

Record of Achievement

I understand that my family are special. ☐

Name ______________________ Date ______________

What does it mean to belong in Christianity?

- Describe what is happening to the baby in the picture.

____

____

- After baptism, the baby in the picture **belongs** to God's family. Draw a picture of something you belong to.

Record of Achievement

I can describe what happens at a baptism service. ☐

Name ______________________________ Date ____________________

What does it mean to belong in Christianity?

- Explain why the person in the picture is pouring water on the baby's head during the baptismal service.

____

____

____

- Why is this person giving a candle to the others?

____

____

____

- Write a sentence that explains what family you belong to after you are baptised.

____

____

Record of Achievement

I can explain some of the events in a baptism service. ☐

Name ______________________ Date ______________

What does it mean to belong in Christianity?

- Write about three important things that happen in a baptism service.

____

____

____

- What is the main reason for being baptised?

____

- What is the name of the person in the bible who baptised people in the River Jordan?

____

- Who was the most important person he baptised?

____

- Draw a picture of what a baptism was like in biblical times.

Record of Achievement

I can explain how and why people are baptised. ☐

Name ______________________ Date ______________

Why do Christians give gifts at Christmas?

- Draw a picture of the Three Wise Men.

- The Wise Men brought gifts for Jesus. Draw and label the three gifts.

Record of Achievement

I can name the Three Wise Men's gifts. ☐

Name ______________________ Date ______________

Why do Christians give gifts at Christmas?

- Look at these pictures of the Three Wise Men's journey.
- Write a sentence for each of the pictures describing their trip to see Jesus.

____

____

____

____

____

____

____

____

____

____

____

____

Record of Achievement

I can tell the story of the Three Wise Men. ☐

Name ______________________ Date ______________

Why do Christians give gifts at Christmas?

- Why do Christians give gifts at Christmas?

____

- What gift do Christians believe God gave to the world?

____

- What qualities do Christians believe Jesus brought to the world? Write some words in the boxes below. The first one has been done for you.

hope

- Choose one of the words and describe it in more detail.

____

____

Record of Achievement

I can describe the qualities Jesus brings to the world. ☐

Name ______________________________ Date ____________________

Why do Christians give gifts at Christmas?

- Draw a picture of a gift you have received this year in the space below.

- How did you feel when you received it? Write a sentence.

____

____

- Draw a picture of a gift you have given somebody this year.

- How did you feel when you gave the gift?

____

____

Record of Achievement

I can describe my feelings. ☐

Name ______________________ Date ______________

Why do Christians give gifts at Christmas?

- Draw and label the three precious gifts that the Wise Men gave Jesus.

- Draw a precious gift you could give to the baby Jesus.

- Write about your gift and why you chose it.

Record of Achievement

I can describe a precious gift.

Name ______________________ Date ______________

Why do Christians give gifts at Christmas?

- Draw and label three gifts you have received this year.

______________ ______________ ______________

- Write a sentence describing your feelings when you received the gifts.

____

____

- Draw a picture of a gift you have given this year.

- Write about your feelings as you gave the person your gift.

____

____

Record of Achievement

I can describe my feelings when giving and receiving gifts. ☐

Name ______________________________ Date ____________________

Beliefs and practice

The religion we have looked at in class is: ____________________

The people who follow this religion believe that

____

____

____

____

They celebrate ____

____

- Draw a religious artefact from this religion.

Record of Achievement

I can write about a key belief from a religion. ☐

Name ______________________ Date ______________

Beliefs and practice

The religion we have looked at in class is: ______________

- Write down two things you have learned about this religion's beliefs.

____

____

- Draw and label a religious artefact associated with this religion.

- Write a sentence explaining when it is used.

____

____

____

Record of Achievement

I can name a religious artefact. ☐

Name ______________________________ Date ________________

Beliefs and practice

The religion we have looked at in class is: ________________

- Draw and label two artefacts associated with this religion.

_______________________ _______________________

- Write a sentence describing what each artefact is used for.

____

____

____

____

- Choose one of the artefacts and write a sentence explaining what it symbolises to the people of that religion.

____

____

Record of Achievement

I can explain the symbolism of a religious artefact. ☐

Name ________________________ Date ________________

How do Jewish people express their beliefs in practice?

- The pictures below show how Moses came to live in the Pharaoh's palace. Write a sentence for each picture telling the story of Moses' early life.

____

____

____

____

____

____

____

____

____

____

____

____

Record of Achievement

I can retell the story of Moses' early life. ☐

Name ______________________________ Date ____________________

How do Jewish people express their beliefs in practice?

- Draw and label three things that happened to Moses during his life.

- Write some sentences describing one of these events in his life.

____

____

____

____

____

____

____

____

Record of Achievement

I can recall some key events in the life of Moses. ☐

Name ______________________________ Date ________________

How do Jewish people express their beliefs in practice?

- Moses was a great leader of the Israelites. Choose one of these events from Moses' life and write a description of it.

____

____

____

____

Record of Achievement

I can explain events that showed Moses as a great leader. ☐

Name ______________________ Date ______________

How do Jewish people express their beliefs in practice?

- Colour the menorah and draw some candles on it.

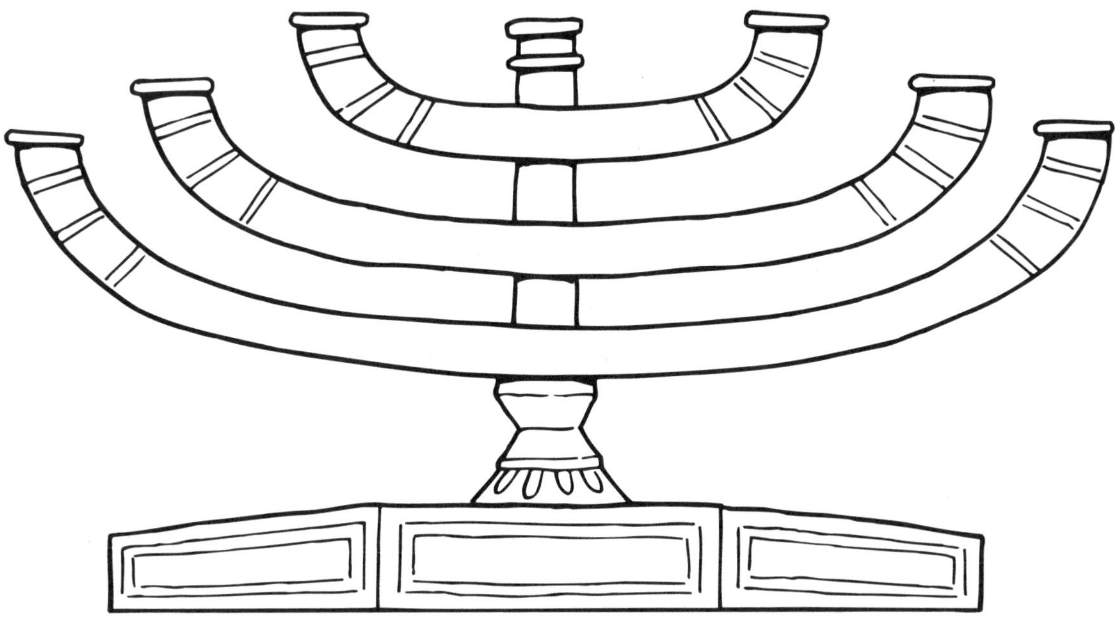

- Choose the correct word to complete the sentence.

The menorah is lit at the Jewish festival of ______________

Passover	Shabbat	Hanukkah

Record of Achievement

I can recognise the feast of Hanukkah. ☐

Name ______________________ Date ______________

How do Jewish people express their beliefs in practice?

This is a ______________________

It is lit at the Jewish festival of Hanukkah.

Hanukkah means festival of ______________________

- Write some things you have learned about the feast of Hanukkah.

____

____

____

____

____

Record of Achievement

I can recognise the key facts about Hanukkah. ☐

Name ______________________ Date ______________

How do Jewish people express their beliefs in practice?

- Draw a picture of a menorah.

- Why does a menorah have seven candles?

___

___

___

- Write about what the Jewish people are remembering at the feast of Hanukkah.

___

___

___

- What special cakes do Jewish people eat at this festival?

___

___

Record of Achievement

I understand the meaning of Hanukkah. ☐

Name ____________________ Date ____________

How do Jewish people express their beliefs in practice?

This family are celebrating the Jewish festival of Passover.

- Write something you have learned about this feast.

____

____

____

____

Record of Achievement

I can recognise the feast of Passover. ☐

Name ____________________ Date ____________

How do Jewish people express their beliefs in practice?

This family are celebrating the Jewish festival of Passover.

- Write down three things you know about this festival.

____

____

____

Record of Achievement

I can recognise the key facts about Passover. ☐

Name ________________________________ Date ____________________

How do Jewish people express their beliefs in practice?

This is the Seder plate. It is used at the Jewish festival of

____

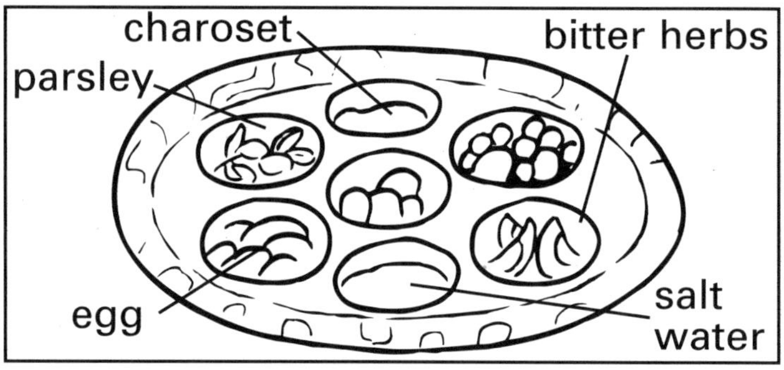

● Each of the foods on the plate reminds the Jewish people of something that happened many years ago. What do the foods below help people to remember?

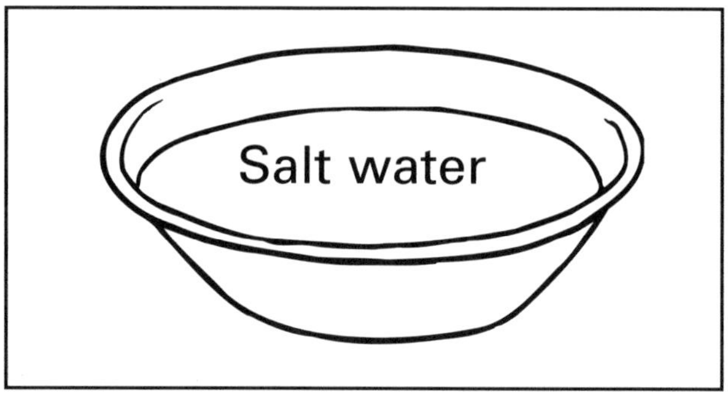

______________________________ ______________________________

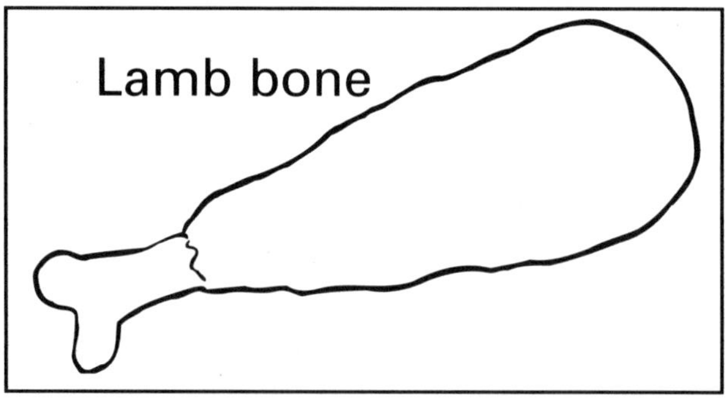

____

Record of Achievement *I understand the meaning of Passover.* ☐

Name ______________________ Date ______________

What can we learn from visiting a church?

- Choose the correct word from the box below to label the pictures correctly.

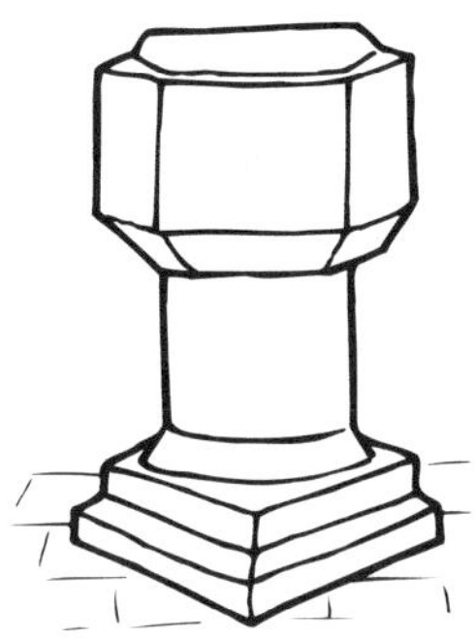

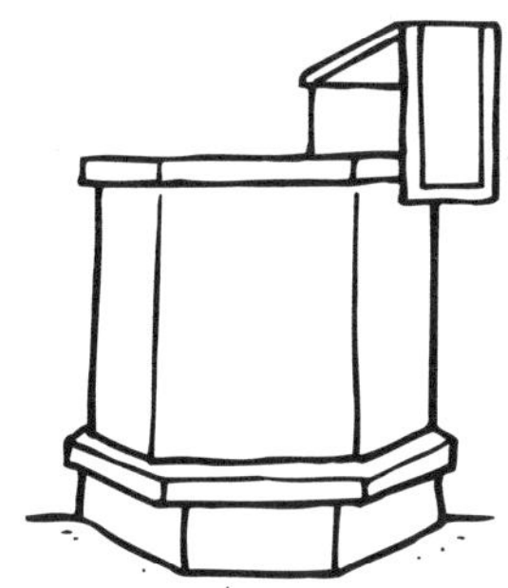

______________ ______________ ______________

pulpit	font	altar	statue	pew	aisle

- Draw a picture of something you have seen in a church. Write the object's name here.

____

Record of Achievement

I can recognise some things found in a church. ☐

Name ______________________ Date ______________

What can we learn from visiting a church?

- Draw and label three things you could find in a church.

____________	____________	____________

- Choose two of the things from the pictures above and explain what they are used for.

____

____

Record of Achievement

I can explain the use of some things found in a church. ☐

Name ______________________ Date ______________

What can we learn from visiting a church?

- Draw a picture of what you think is an important feature in a church.

- Explain why this feature is important for Christians.

- Make a list of words that would describe the atmosphere in a church.

- Draw an event that takes place in a church.

Record of Achievement

I can describe the atmosphere in a church.

PSHE and citizenship

As there are no QCA guidelines for PSHE, the worksheets for this subject have been selected to address what we feel is covered by most schools under 'PSHE time'. The citizenship worksheets are based on the QCA's Scheme of Work. In Year 1, children are introduced to the idea of rights and responsibilities and the role they can play within that. They are also encouraged to consider the role of professionals within the community, such as the police force. Of the six units available, Units 3 and 4 have been chosen for study.

It is important to remember that many of the issues covered in this section are potentially sensitive, and will need to be handled with care. Discussion with children will need to be carefully handled, particularly with relevance to work on 'keeping safe'.

Growing and changing

✔ **Learning outcome** (page 149)
To understand that we change as we grow.

✔✔ **Learning outcome** (page 150)
To understand that what we can do changes as we grow.

✔✔✔ **Learning outcome** (page 151)
To understand that the process of growing and changing has many consequences.

By identifying their own physical growth and change, children should come to understand what effect their growth has on them and their abilities. Ask the children to think about (or ask an adult about) when they were babies – can they do anything now that they couldn't do then? Ask children with younger siblings to think about how they differ from them and how the younger child needs more looking after.

Children should become familiar with words that describe growth (*size, shape, tall, short, bigger, growing*) and allow them to make comparisons (*same, different*) and to talk about family (*brother, sister, parent, family*).

The worksheets in this unit require the children to have discussed things they could do when they were babies in terms of movement, speech and independence, and to be able to compare this with what they can do now. It's important to discuss who has helped them grow and how these people have helped them. Children will need to understand that as they grow and change they will have different requirements in terms of clothes and food and so on. Photocopiable page 149 encourages the children to think about how they are growing and changing, and how this affects what they are able to do. This is extended on photocopiable page 150 to look at specific activities that babies can and can't do, and how their abilities will change over time. Children who complete photocopiable page 151 should consider specific ways in which their bodies are growing, and how this affects their abilities.

Keeping safe

✔ **Learning outcome** (page 152)
To understand that certain things in the home can lead to danger.

✔✔ **Learning outcome** (page 153)
To understand how and why things can be dangerous.

✔✔✔ **Learning outcome** (page 154)
To know how to keep safe indoors and outdoors.

These activities will help the children to become aware of the need for safety and to think about how they can protect themselves. Talk about things around the home that could lead to danger if not treated with respect. You might like to give children the opportunity to talk about their own experiences; perhaps if someone has avoided an accident they could explain how they kept safe. Any discussion like this will need to be handled with care – it is important to emphasise how children should share the responsibility for their safety with others.

When working on this unit, ensure the children have become familiar with certain words and phrases, for example *dangerous, safe, rules, harm.*

It will be useful for the children to discuss safety at times when they may be on their own outside the home. This should include discussion on adults we should ask for help and those we shouldn't. Photocopiable page 152 focuses on children identifying potential dangers and thinking about why they might be dangerous. Pages 153 and 154 ask children to identify dangers inside and outside the home, and to think about how they could keep themselves safe from these.

Animals and us

Unit 3

✔ **Learning outcome** (page 155)
To know that we have a responsibility to care for animals.

✔✔ **Learning outcomes** (page 156)
To understand that humans have a responsibility to all animals. To know to contact a vet when an animal is ill.

Through identifying the basic needs of animals, the children will develop their own understanding of how it is their responsibility to protect animals and consider how they can go about this.

They will be using words such as *needs, rights, care, rules, responsibility, pets, wildlife, farm* and *animals.*

On photocopiable page 155 children identify pets and wild creatures and consider ways to care for them. Photocopiable

✔✔✔ Learning outcomes (page 157)
To appreciate that humans have a responsibility towards all animals. To know how to protect wildlife.

page 156 compares humans to animals, helping the children to learn that some basic needs are similar and that it is our duty to care for animals as well as ourselves. The sheet also identifies who to contact if an animal is ill. Photocopiable page 157 introduces the idea of rules for animal care, particularly wildlife, linking to the environment and knowledge of organisations that are concerned with animal welfare.

People who help us – the local police

Unit 4

✔ Learning outcomes (page 158)
To name parts of a police uniform. To know how to ask for help.
✔✔ Learning outcomes (page 159)
To recognise that people who help us sometimes wear uniform. To know how to get help in an emergency.
✔✔✔ Learning outcomes (page 160)
To describe the purpose of some parts of a police uniform. To describe ways a police officer can help. To know how to contact the police in an emergency.

In this section, through considering the role of the police in the local community, children will come to understand how police officers can help them and those around them. The children are given the opportunity to consider strategies for keeping safe and how to deal with situations in which they may be at risk.

When completing these worksheets, ensure the children become familiar with words and phrases about people who help us, for example *police, teacher, fire officer, nurse, doctor,* and words that are associated with danger, such as *risk, rules, responsibility, safety.*

Photocopiable page 158 requires children to develop an awareness of the local police, parts of their uniform and some of the work they do. This is developed on photocopiable pages 159 and 160, where the children also identify other people who help us and suggest ways in which they can be contacted in an emergency.

Name ______________________ Date ______________

Growing and changing

● Draw someone older than you.	● Draw someone younger than you.	● Draw a picture of yourself.

● Write about one thing you couldn't do as a baby.

____

____

____

● Write about one thing you can't do now but you will be able to do when you are bigger.

____

____

____

Record of Achievement

I understand that I am growing and changing. ☐

Name ______________________________ Date ________________

Growing and changing

- Draw a ring round the things a baby can't do.

crawl

cry

ride a bike

go to school

drive a car

write in a book

feed from a bottle

- Draw something you can do.

- Draw something you will be able to do when you are bigger.

Record of Achievement

I understand that there are some things we can only do when we are bigger. ☐

Name ______________________ Date ______________

Growing and changing

Which parts of your body are growing? How do you know? Draw and write about four parts of you that are growing and what it means.

My hands  **I had to have new gloves.** 

Record of Achievement

I can say what happens when some parts of our bodies grow and change. ☐

Name ______________________ Date ______________

Keeping safe

- Put a ring round the things that could be dangerous.

- Draw one more thing that could be dangerous.

- Why might this thing be dangerous? Write a sentence.

____

____

____

Record of Achievement

I can identify things that could be dangerous. ☐

Name ______________________________ Date ____________________

Keeping safe

- Draw and label four things that could be dangerous.

____________________	____________________
____________________	____________________

- Choose one of the things you have drawn and write a sentence saying how it could be dangerous.

____

____

- How could you keep yourself safe from it?

____

____

Record of Achievement *I can identify things that could be dangerous and say why.* ☐

Name ____________________ Date ____________

Keeping safe

- Draw and label two things that can be dangerous inside your home.

- Draw and label two things that can be dangerous outside.

- Choose one of the indoor dangers and write a sentence saying how to keep yourself safe from it.

- Choose one of the outdoor dangers and write a sentence saying how to keep yourself safe from it.

Record of Achievement

I can identify dangerous things indoors and outdoors and say how to keep safe from them. ☐

Name ______________________ Date ______________

Animals and us

- Draw an animal it would be suitable to keep as a pet.

- Write three ways you would make sure your pet was properly cared for.

____

____

____

- Draw three wild animals that live in the school grounds or your garden.

- Write two ways you could look after these animals.

____

____

Record of Achievement

I know that humans must care for animals properly. ☐

Name ______________________________ Date ____________________

Animals and us

Humans and animals need certain things to be happy and healthy.

- List some things you and your animal need to be happy and healthy.

Me	Cat
food	*food*

- Put a ring around the person you would take to if your animal was ill.

doctor vet police officer

fire officer teacher

Record of Achievement

I can recognise that animals need to be looked after. ☐

Name ______________________ Date ______________

Animals and us

- Humans have a responsibility to protect wild animals. Draw two wild animals that can be found in the school grounds and write about why they are important.

- Make up a list of rules for a wildlife area.

Record of Achievement

I know that it is important to protect wild animals. I can suggest ways in which they can be protected. ☐

Name ______________________ Date ______________

People who help us – the local police

- Draw someone who helps us who doesn't wear a uniform.

- Write three things that they do.

____

____

____

- Draw and label three parts of a police officer's uniform.

- Write two ways that a police officer help us.

____

____

- How would you get help from a police officer?

____

____

____

Record of Achievement

I can name some parts of a police officer's uniform.
I know how to ask for help. ☐

Name ______________________ Date ______________

People who help us – the local police

- List three people who help us who **do not** wear uniforms.

____

____

____

- List three people who help us who **do** wear uniforms.

____

____

____

- Label the different parts of a police officer's uniform.

- Give one reason why a police officer might come into school.

____

- What would you do if you needed a police officer in an emergency?

____

Record of Achievement

I recognise that some people who help us wear uniform. I can name some parts of a police officer's uniform. I know how to get help in an emergency. ☐

Name ______________________ Date ______________

People who help us – the local police

- Draw two parts of a police officer's uniform and explain what they are for.

[ ]	____________________
[ ]	____________________

- Write about the how a police officer could help you.

____

- Write about how a police officer could help Mum or Dad.

____

- How do you contact the police in an emergency?

____

____

Record of Achievement

I know the functions of some parts of a police uniform.
I can describe different ways the police can help people.
I know how to contact them in an emergency. ☐